The Silent
and
The Cave

Wasyl Nimenko

Goalpath Books

The Silent Guru and the Cave

ISBN 978-1-908142-66-5

Published in Great Britain 2023

Goalpath Books

Wasyl Nimenko was born in Ipswich and studied medicine in London then psychotherapy.

Also by Wasyl Nimenko

Fiction   Invisible Bullets

Non-Fiction   Acceptance and Meaning in Grief
                 Carl Jung and Ramana Maharshi
                 Searching in Secret Ukraine
                 Notes from the Inside
                 The Spiritual Nature of Addictions

Travel   Searching in Secret Orkney
                 Searching in Secret India
                 Searching in Secret New Zealand and
                 Australia

Poems   The Fools Poems Part 1
                 The Fools Poems Part 11

The Silent Guru
and
The Cave

Goalpath Books

Like Groundhog Day, it can seem that repeated effort keeps on returning us to the same place. But with perseverance, eventually we see who we are.

CONTENTS

1.

The Sage

Like Groundhog Day, it can seem that repeated effort keeps on returning us to the same place. But with perseverance, eventually we see who we are.

The boy was tired. It had been a long afternoon of walking. As he approached a crossroads he could see there were no signs. He was looking for somewhere to stay the night to break his journey south.

A group of three men were talking just a few yards down the right hand turning. They stopped talking as he approached. He felt much younger than them but decided to ask them if there was somewhere to stay the night.

'Are there rooms or a hostel to stay nearby?

'Nothing around here.' Said the broadest man.

'How far until there is one?'

'Half a day's journey straight on to the next village.' Said the tallest of the three men.

'So there is nothing else?'

'No.' said the tall man again. The other men nodded in agreement. 'Not unless you want to stay the night with the beggars in an old graveyard."

'No.' The boy said. But to his surprise he kept looking at the tall man, as if the man hadn't finished and had something else to say.

'Nothing other than that.' The tall man said. 'You will have to walk fast to get to the next village before the light goes.'

'How far is the graveyard?'

'An hour and a half.' Turn left just here and it's towards the hills. The road ends and there's nothing. It's arid land. But if you keep walking straight, eventually you'll see some old gravestones. No one goes there. They say only beggars live there.'

Two hours later the boy came to the end of the road. There was just a gentle rise in the ground towards the hills over the next half a mile. He stopped and looked around. Here there was nothing except the occasional slightly raised areas of ground. He thought these must be the old graves the men mentioned.

The area looked as if it was not tended by any relatives of the people buried there. There were some low laying shrubs between some of the trees which were about every thirty yards apart. He guessed that there couldn't be more than about

thirty to forty people buried here in this graveyard.

Apart from the graves, the only evidence that man had marked this area was a small building he could see in the distance at the far end of the graveyard. Now that he had arrived, the boy was more interested in sitting under the shade of a tree to rest his body from the walking. He put his bag against a tree, sat resting his back against it and fell into a deep sleep.

◎

The boy woke in the darkness looking up at the stars which now surrounded him. He could see there was a light in the distance and it was coming towards him. As the light got closer to him he could see it was a lamp being carried by a man.

He sat motionless in case the man with the light hadn't noticed him and would walk on. Was it the beggar the men had mentioned? Slowly and quite definitely someone was moving towards him.

He wondered if the beggar had spotted him or if this was just the usual path they used. The boy sat still and waited. But he felt uncomfortable sitting so he stood up waiting for the light to approach him closer. Eventually it stopped several yards from him.

From behind the light of the oil lamp the man's hand beckoned him to follow.

'I was travelling south. I was too tired to carry on so

I was looking for a hostel to stay a night. I was told this was the nearest place I might be able to stay. Is it ok to stay?' said the boy.

The old man didn't speak.

The boy followed the man back to where the light had first appeared in the direction of the building he had noticed before he had fallen asleep.

When they entered the building, the boy noticed there was no other light apart from the light from the oil lamp which the old man held and which he now placed on the floor. Against the wall were some hessian cushions. The boy noticed a table but otherwise the room seemed empty.

The old man handed the boy a bowl of soup and a cup of water and pointed to the hessian cushions and the boy knew this was his bed. It was home for the night.

The boy felt he had arrived somewhere very strange and also that the man was strange. He had not even spoken. Then he realised the man had communicated everything perfectly in silence.

◎

The boy woke to rays of early morning sunlight reflected off the white painted walls and the shiny stone floor of the room which now seemed simple, clean and comfortable. He sat up to see the old man facing a window.

The old man was sitting still with his eyes closed facing the hills through the window. The boy watched him and became aware that the man seemed to radiate a peacefulness which brought the boys mind to a state of being very conscious of his thoughts. It was as if the old man was showing him something and he was inviting him to follow his example.

After some time sitting still looking at the old man the boy noticed the old man open his eyes. He looked straight ahead out of the window at the hills. After some more time he spoke.

'Why you are here?'

'As I said last night, I was just looking for a place to stay the night. I am on my way south. It seems very peaceful here.'

'There is no more peaceful place than inside your self.'

The man was still for some time. Then he asked the boy, 'Who are you?'

'I am from up north of the river. I am travelling south looking for a better life. My family are unhappy and make me unhappy. The world of business they are connected to doesn't interest me at all. I am looking for something deeper, with meaning. For true happiness.'

'These are the two questions which you should ask every day at the beginning of your day.' There was a pause almost as if he wanted the boy to remember.

'The answer to Why am I here is this. It is to find the happiness which is inside you.' He paused again, once more so as if that the boy could remember what he had said.

'The answer to the Who am I is this. You find out by finding out what you are not. You say you are not this and not that. You are not your thoughts. You are not a collection of thoughts which is called the ego.' He paused again as if to let the boy absorb what he had said.

'What is really you is not your body. It is not your memories or your thoughts about the future. You are simply consciousness without thoughts.' He paused again.

'What has always been there aware of all your thoughts is your consciousness. It is what sees without eyes, what hears without ears. That is what you are.' There was one last pause, the longest.

'Seeing that you are this consciousness of everything, which is the same as the consciousness of the universe, you eventually see this is in truth what you are. So you must actually be it.

'Every morning when you sit in stillness ask, Why am I here? The answer is to be happy inside. Then ask, Who am I? The answer is realised by seeing what you are not. I am not this, not that. I am consciousness. I am that I am, which is everything. I am that.'

'How do you know this?' The boy asked.

'It is what I studied and practiced my whole life. It is the art of being happy by looking within for happiness.'

'You are here as an old man, alone. Does it work?'

'Yes. But that is enough. If you want to know more I will have to tell you tomorrow. I must go and get some food.'

The old man got up and took a hessian bag with him as he walked out of the door towards the direction of the road.

When the old man had gone the boy took out a pencil and a notebook and wrote down what the man had told him.

◎

The next morning the boy was once again woken by the rays of sunlight reflecting off the walls and the shiny floor.

The old man was sitting still with his eyes closed facing the hills through the window. The boy watched him and became aware that the man seemed to radiate a peacefulness which brought the boys mind to a state of being very conscious of his thoughts. It was as if the old

7

man was showing him something and he was inviting him to follow his example.

When the old man opened his eyes from looking out the window, as he had done the day before, he turned to the boy and spoke again.

'Every morning when you sit in stillness ask, Why am I here? The answer is to be happy inside. Then ask, Who am I? The answer is realised by seeing what you are not. I am not this, not that. I am consciousness. I am that I am, which is everything. I am that.'

∞

'The ancient civilisations knew it. They knew that happiness was inside. In Judaism, when Moses asked God for his name he answered, "I Am That I Am. Thus shalt you say unto the children of Israel, I Am has sent me to you." Jehovah means I am. So knowing the self, God is known as they are taken to be the same.' He paused.

∞

'The Pashupati Seal is a soapstone seal discovered at the Mohenjo-daro archaeological site of the Indus Valley Civilisation. It is estimated to have been carved around 2350 BC and is thought to be the earliest prototype of the God Shiva. The seal shows a seated cross-legged figure in the yogic 'padmasama' or lotus meditation posture with arms pointing downwards. It is important because it is one of the first communications from our ancient ancestors which reflects the stillness of silently looking inwards.'

∞

'In Hinduism the mind is helped to look inwards by "Netti Netti," from the Brihadaranyaka Upanishad written around 800 BC, meaning, "Neither this neither that," which helps the mind to constantly disidentify with anything other than that which is everything.'

∞

'One of the ancient Greek's key instructions, "Know the self." was written on the portals of their most important temple, the Temple of Apollo in Delphi.'

∞

'In the Hebrew Bible or the Tanaka, in Psalm 46, God is assumed to be inside, "Be still and know that I am God."

∞

'And again in Christianity in Luke 17, it says, "The kingdom of God is within you." Do you see it?'

∞

'Even Shakespeare pointed man strongly inside,' "This above all-to thine own self be true."

∞

'So you see, they all say that happiness is inside. We have to be that consciousness not just in the morning when we sit still. But gradually we become that consciousness 'I Am' more and more throughout the day. We surrender to it. We surrender our Self to the Universe. Then we become it.'

'How do you know this?' The boy asked.

'It is what I studied and practiced my whole life. It is the art of being happy by looking within for happiness.'

'If you want to know more I will have to tell you tomorrow. I must go and get some food.'

The old man got up and took a hessian bag with him as he walked out of the door towards the direction of the road.

When the old man had gone the boy took out a pencil and a notebook and wrote down what the man had told him.

◎

The next morning the boy was once again woken by the rays of sunlight reflecting off the walls and the shiny floor.

The old man was sitting still with his eyes closed facing the hills through the window. The boy watched him and became aware that the man seemed to radiate a peacefulness which brought the boys mind to a state of being very conscious of his thoughts. It was as if the old man was showing him something and he was inviting him to follow his example.

When the old man opened his eyes from looking out the window, as he had done the day before, he turned to the boy and spoke again.

'Every morning when you sit in stillness ask, Why am I here? The answer is to be happy inside. Then ask, Who am I? The answer is realised by seeing what you are not. I am not this, not that. I am consciousness. I am that I am, which is everything. I am that.'

∞

10

'Happiness can't be acquired like a possession. You may have looked at acquiring money, things, power, influence or knowledge to make you happy. You may have looked at having all of these possessions to make you happy. But these will make you bored and you will endlessly keep going onto the next best thing. Possessions lead to fear of their use and loss. Fear and loss make us think we will be happier if we can more securely possess them, so an endless pursuit begins. Loss anxiety makes us try harder to possess what does not even make us happy.'

∞

'Don't be misled by beauty because Beauty is something recognised outside, happiness is always inside. Beauty is derived from the senses, happiness is revealed inside. Beauty is a synthesis of fine thinking, happiness is simply being in the heart with no thoughts.'

∞

'There is no relationship between any form of possession and happiness.'

∞

'How do we know this? A powerful wealthy influential person will always have loss anxiety about their securities. They cannot be as happy as the person who has found happiness inside. Seeing that acquiring things, money, power, influence or knowledge does not make you happy, there is only one place left to look for happiness. Inside.'

'How do you know this?' The boy asked.

'It is what I studied and practiced my whole life. It

is the art of being happy by looking within for happiness.'

'You are here as an old man, alone. Does it work?'

'Yes. But that is enough. If you want to know more I will have to tell you tomorrow. I must go and get some food.'

The old man got up and took a hessian bag with him as he walked out of the door towards the direction of the road.

When the old man had gone the boy took out a pencil and a notebook and wrote down what the man had told him.

◎

The next morning the boy was once again woken by the rays of sunlight reflecting off the walls and the shiny floor.

The old man was sitting still with his eyes closed facing the hills through the window. The boy watched him and became aware that the man seemed to radiate a peacefulness which brought the boys mind to a state of being very conscious of his thoughts. It was as if the old man was showing him something and he was inviting him to follow his example.

When the old man opened his eyes from looking out the window, as he had done the day before, he turned to the boy and spoke again.

'Every morning when you sit in stillness ask, Why am I here? The answer is to be happy inside. Then ask, Who am I? The answer is realised by seeing what you are not. I am not this, not that. I am consciousness. I am that I am, which is everything. I am that.'

∞

'To be happy you need to see you can't acquire it by adding something to yourself. Instead, see that you have to remove something about you. Get rid of your belief that you can acquire happiness by seeing you already have it.'

∞

'Happiness is seen by getting rid of looking outside of you for happiness.'

∞

'Happiness is seen by getting rid of thinking security of any kind will make you happy.'

∞

'Happiness is seen by getting rid of searching for happiness because it is already inside you.'

∞

'Happiness is seen by constant effort to be happy.'

∞

'Happiness is experienced by seeing happiness is not hidden but that you have just been looking outside for happiness when all along it is inside.'

'How do you know this?' The boy asked.

'It is what I studied and practiced my whole life. It is the art of being happy by looking within for happiness.'

'You are here as an old man, alone. Does it work?'

'Yes. But that is enough. If you want to know more

I will have to tell you tomorrow. I must go and get some food.'

The old man got up and took a hessian bag with him as he walked out of the door towards the direction of the road.

When the old man had gone the boy took out a pencil and a notebook and wrote down what the man had told him.

◎

The next morning the boy was once again woken by the rays of sunlight reflecting off the walls and the shiny floor.

The old man was sitting still with his eyes closed facing the hills through the window. The boy watched him and became aware that the man seemed to radiate a peacefulness which brought the boys mind to a state of being very conscious of his thoughts. It was as if the old man was showing him something and he was inviting him to follow his example.

When the old man opened his eyes from looking out the window, as he had done the day before, he turned to the boy and spoke again.

'Every morning when you sit in stillness ask, Why am I here? The answer is to be happy inside. Then ask, Who am I? The answer is realised by seeing what you are not. I am not this, not that. I am consciousness. I am that I am, which is everything. I am that.'

∞

'You can only ever be happy today, only in the present, only today, only right now.'

∞

'You can only be happy today, in the present, right now, so give up the search in the future, so you can see it now.'

∞

'Happiness is inside and we can only be happy right now today.

∞

'To access happiness we have to get rid of thinking it is outside or in the future.'

∞

'Like light is always here from the sun but we may be busy looking at something else; we only need to turn inside to see our happiness.'

∞

'We may not be able to be happy all the time but our happiness is always here inside us.'

∞

'Your happiness depends on seeing your happiness is already inside you and is not something new which can be acquired from outside.'

'How do you know this?' The boy asked.

'It is what I studied and practiced my whole life. It

is the art of being happy by looking within for happiness.'

'You are here as an old man, alone. Does it work?'

'Yes. But that is enough. If you want to know more I will have to tell you tomorrow. I must go and get some food.'

The old man got up and took a hessian bag with him as he walked out of the door towards the direction of the road.

When the old man had gone the boy took out a pencil and a notebook and wrote down what the man had told him.

◎

The next morning the boy was once again woken by the rays of sunlight reflecting off the walls and the shiny floor.

The old man was sitting still with his eyes closed facing the hills through the window. The boy watched him and became aware that the man seemed to radiate a peacefulness which brought the boys mind to a state of being very conscious of his thoughts. It was as if the old man was showing him something and he was inviting him to follow his example.

When the old man opened his eyes from looking out the window, as he had done the day before, he turned to the boy and spoke again.

'Every morning when you sit in stillness ask, Why am I here? The answer is to be happy inside. Then ask, Who am I? The answer is realised by seeing what you are not. I am not this, not that. I am consciousness. I am that I am, which is everything. I am that.'

∞

16

'To be happy now, you have to be happy with what you are, with what you have.'

∞

'To be happy with what you are and what you have is to be happy with just sufficient.'

∞

'Sufficient is what is enough. Enough for how long? Well today is how long.'

'How do you know this?' The boy asked.

'It is what I studied and practiced my whole life. It is the art of being happy by looking within for happiness.'

'You are here as an old man, alone. Does it work?'

'Yes. But that is enough. If you want to know more I will have to tell you tomorrow. I must go and get some food.'

The old man got up and took a hessian bag with him as he walked out of the door towards the direction of the road.

When the old man had gone the boy took out a pencil and a notebook and wrote down what the man had told him.

◎

The next morning the boy was once again woken by the rays of sunlight reflecting off the walls and the shiny floor.

The old man was sitting still with his eyes closed facing the hills through the window. The boy watched him and became aware that the man seemed to radiate a peacefulness which brought the boys mind to a state of being very conscious of his thoughts. It was as if the old man was showing him something and he was inviting him to follow his example.

When the old man opened his eyes from looking out the window, as he had done the day before, he turned to the boy and spoke again.

'Every morning when you sit in stillness ask, Why am I here? The answer is to be happy inside. Then ask, Who am I? The answer is realised by seeing what you are not. I am not this, not that. I am consciousness. I am that I am, which is everything. I am that.'

∞

'When you see you are as happy as you can be today without wanting anything, you have found happiness. When you see this you see you have no want. When you see you have no want you cannot be happier. Do you know a person with no want?'

∞

'The easiest way to make yourself an exile from your happiness is to start thinking about what you want in the future.'

∞

'There are only three things we don't see about happiness. The first is that to access happiness we have to get rid of thinking it is outside. Like light is always here from the sun but we may be busy looking at something else; we only need to turn inside to see our happiness. We may not be able to be happy all the time but our

18

happinessisalwayshereinsideus. Yourhappinessdependson seeing your happiness is already inside you and is not something new which can be acquired from outside.'

∞

'The second is that you can't actually ever be happy tomorrow, only today. You can only be happy today, in the present, right now, so give up the search in the future, so you can see it now. Happiness is inside and we can only be happy right now today.'

∞

'The third is that to be happy now, you have to be happy with what you have and have no want. To be happy with what you are and what you have is to be happy with just sufficient. Sufficient is what is enough. Enough for how long? Well today is how long.'

'How do you know this?' The boy asked.

'It is what I studied and practiced my whole life. It is the art of being happy by looking within for happiness.'

'You are here as an old man, alone. Does it work?'

'Yes. But that is enough. If you want to know more I will have to tell you tomorrow. I must go and get some food.'

The old man got up and took a hessian bag with him as he walked out of the door towards the direction of the road.

When the old man had gone the boy took out a pencil and a notebook and wrote down what the man had told him.

◎

The next morning the boy was once again woken by the rays of sunlight reflecting off the walls and the shiny floor.

The old man was sitting still with his eyes closed facing the hills through the window. The boy watched him and became aware that the man seemed to radiate a peacefulness which brought the boys mind to a state of being very conscious of his thoughts. It was as if the old man was showing him something and he was inviting him to follow his example.

When the old man opened his eyes from looking out the window, as he had done the day before, he turned to the boy and spoke again.

'Every morning when you sit in stillness ask, Why am I here? The answer is to be happy inside. Then ask, Who am I? The answer is realised by seeing what you are not. I am not this, not that. I am consciousness. I am that I am, which is everything. I am that.'

∞

'Seeing our goal is inner stillness, we try to use thinking to find it but we can only find our stillness by being still, not by thinking about it.'

∞

'When we look inside at 'Who are we?' we become conscious we are not thought.'

'It is a surprise to discover that you are not your thoughts, which through meditation seem like imposters.'

∞

'We are taught and programmed to believe we are a

bundle of thoughts called the ego.'

∞

'But in meditation you see you are not just a bundle of thoughts.'

∞

'When you stay with this you begin to see consciousness comes before thought. Consciousness is always here. Thought comes and goes.'

∞

'In meditation you see you are consciousness which is not a thought but is what creates thought.'

∞

'There is no more mystery.'

∞

'There is no more misery about our thinking.'

∞

'In wanting to see what we are, it is essential to ask and find out what we are not.'

∞

'We think we are our memories, but these are just

21

thoughts, so if we believe this, we can easily take ourselves to be what we are not. We may think we are what we imagine in the future but this is just thought and is not what we are now.'

∞

'In asking what you are and what you are not, you see you are not your thoughts but consciousness, which is responsible for thoughts.'

∞

'When something is made up it has no authenticity; just as you always know when an actor is acting.'

∞

'The same mistaken authenticity is obvious when our ignorance of believing we are the ego is uncovered.'

∞

'You can see what you are is consciousness of stillness inside you.'

∞

'Consciousness of inner stillness lets us see our inner self is stillness.'

∞

'Consciousness of inner stillness lets us see that our

inner self is our natural happiness.'

∞

'Our answer to what we are is I am just 'I am,' the consciousness we all have of inner stillness.'

'How do you know this?' The boy asked.

'It is what I studied and practiced my whole life. It is the art of being happy by looking within for happiness.'

'You are here as an old man, alone. Does it work?'

'Yes. But that is enough. If you want to know more I will have to tell you tomorrow. I must go and get some food.'

The old man got up and took a hessian bag with him as he walked out of the door towards the direction of the road.

When the old man had gone the boy took out a pencil and a notebook and wrote down what the man had told him.

◎

The next morning the boy was once again woken by the rays of sunlight reflecting off the walls and the shiny floor.

The old man was sitting still with his eyes closed facing the hills through the window. The boy watched him and became aware that the man seemed to radiate a peacefulness which brought the boys mind to a state of being very conscious of his thoughts. It was as if the old man was showing him something and he was inviting him to follow his example.

When the old man opened his eyes from looking out the window, as he had done the day before, he turned to the boy and spoke again.

'Every morning when you sit in stillness ask, Why am I here? The answer is to be happy inside. Then ask, Who am I? The answer is realised by seeing what you are not. I am not this, not that. I am consciousness. I am that I am, which is everything. I am that.'

∞

'When we see what the world is like and that what we do doesn't work, we realise that to be our inner self, we have to surrender to what we trust.'

∞

'What we trust is either inside us or outside us.'

∞

'The first path may be to look inside and enquire into what is our nature and to surrender to that.'

∞

'The other path is to look to something outside us. It can be a place of pilgrimage, a mountain, a god or a saint. Then surrender to that.'

∞

'Whichever path we take, we eventually see we have surrendered to our inner self.'

∞

'When we see this we can keep or withdraw the projection but it makes no difference as all is seen as one.'

'How do you know this?' The boy asked.

'It is what I studied and practiced my whole life. It is the art of being happy by looking within for happiness.'

'You are here as an old man, alone. Does it work?'

'Yes. But that is enough. If you want to know more I will have to tell you tomorrow. I must go and get some food.'

The old man got up and took a hessian bag with him as he walked out of the door towards the direction of the road.

When the old man had gone the boy took out a pencil and a notebook and wrote down what the man had told him.

◎

The next morning the boy was once again woken by the rays of sunlight reflecting off the walls and the shiny floor.

The old man was sitting still with his eyes closed facing the hills through the window. The boy watched him and became aware that the man seemed to radiate a peacefulness which brought the boys mind to a state of being very conscious of his thoughts. It was as if the old man was showing him something and he was inviting him to follow his example.

When the old man opened his eyes from looking out the window, as he had done the day before, he turned to the boy and spoke again.

'Every morning when you sit in stillness ask, Why am I here? The answer is to be happy inside. Then ask, Who am I? The answer is realised by seeing what you are not. I am not this, not that. I am consciousness. I am that I

25

am, which is everything. I am that.'

∞

'We are not born unhappy but our circumstances make us unhappy, so we try to find the happiness we know is inside. This is our nature.'

∞

'Our happiness is our self which is the same as everything in the Universe and no different from it.'

∞

'Religions point to seeing our inner self as our higher power inside as God. Most simply this is consciousness of "I am." This can be seen in the words from the east and the west over the last three thousand years. Let me remind you of what I said the ancients knew before I bring you to the modern age.'

∞

'When Moses asked God for his name he answered,' "I Am That I Am. Thus shalt you say unto the children of Israel, I Am has sent me to you." 'Jehovah means I am. So knowing the self, God is known as they are taken to be the same.'

∞

''Netti Netti' means, "Neither this neither this," 'Which helps the mind to constantly disidentify with

26

anything other than that which is everything.

∞

"Know the self." 'Comes from the Temple of
Apollo, in Delphi in Greece.'

∞

"Be still and know that I am God," 'Is from Psalm
46.' "The kingdom of God is within you," 'Is from Luke.'

∞

'Over a thousand years ago an Indian Guru
called Shankara wrote in a series of verses called
Vivekachudamani,' "Even after the Truth has been
realised, there remains that strong, obstinate impression that
one is still an ego - the agent and experiencer. This has to be
carefully removed by living in a state of constant
identification with the supreme non-dual Self. Full
Awakening is the eventual ceasing of all the mental im-
pressions of being an ego."

∞

"This above all-to thine own self be true," 'Was
written by Shakespeare.'

∞

'All of this was most clearly summarised by
another Indian Guru, Ramana Maharshi when he said
in 1937, "Your duty is to be and not to be this or that. 'I

27

AM that I AM' sums up the whole truth. The method is summarised in 'Be still.' What does 'stillness' mean? It means 'destroy yourself.' Because any form or shape is the cause of trouble. Give up the notion that, I am so and so."

∞

'Again going back to Shankara, he also said this about the ego and the self. "The fool takes the reflection of the sun in the water of a pot to be the sun; the wise man eliminates pot, water, and reflection and knows the sun in the sky as it really is, single and unaffected, but illuminating all three. In the same way the fool through error and misperception, identifies himself with the ego and its reflected light experienced through the medium of the intellect. The wise and discriminating man eliminates body, intellect, and reflected light of consciousness and probes deeply into his real Self which illuminates all three while remaining uniform in the ether of the heart. Thereby he realises the eternal witness which is absolute knowledge, illuminating all three."

'How do you know this?' The boy asked.

'It is what I studied and practiced my whole life. It is the art of being happy by looking within for happiness.'

'You are here as an old man, alone. Does it work?'

'Yes. But that is enough. If you want to know more I will have to tell you tomorrow. I must go and get some food.'

The old man got up and took a hessian bag with him as he walked out of the door towards the direction of the road.

When the old man had gone the boy took out a pencil and a notebook and wrote down what the man had told him.

The next morning the boy was once again woken by the rays of sunlight reflecting off the walls and the shiny floor.

The old man was sitting still with his eyes closed facing the hills through the window. The boy watched him and became aware that the man seemed to radiate a peacefulness which brought the boys mind to a state of being very conscious of his thoughts. It was as if the old man was showing him something and he was inviting him to follow his example.

When the old man opened his eyes from looking out the window, as he had done the day before, he turned to the boy and spoke again.

'Every morning when you sit in stillness ask, Why am I here? The answer is to be happy inside. Then ask, Who am I? The answer is realised by seeing what you are not. I am not this, not that. I am consciousness. I am that I am, which is everything. I am that.'

∞

'Meditation is turning inwards to find inner happiness.'

∞

'When we see what we are our searching ends.'

∞

'Somehow we discover that between our thoughts, is our inner stillness.'

'Whatever way we reach this stillness and surrender to it, is our own meditation, our own truth.'

∞

'How do you know this?' The boy asked.

'It is what I studied and practiced my whole life. It is the art of being happy by looking within for happiness.'

'You are here as an old man, alone. Does it work?'

'Yes. But that is enough. If you want to know more I will have to tell you tomorrow. I must go and get some food.'

The old man got up and took a hessian bag with him as he walked out of the door towards the direction of the road.

When the old man had gone the boy took out a pencil and a notebook and wrote down what the man had told him.

◎

The next morning the boy was once again woken by the rays of sunlight reflecting off the walls and the shiny floor.

The old man was sitting still with his eyes closed facing the hills through the window. The boy watched him and became aware that the man seemed to radiate a peacefulness which brought the boys mind to a state of being very conscious of his thoughts. It was as if the old man was showing him something and he was inviting him to follow his example.

When the old man opened his eyes from looking out the window, as he had done the day before, he turned to the boy and spoke again.

'Every morning when you sit in stillness ask, Why am I here? The answer is to be happy inside. Then ask, Who am I? The answer is realised by seeing what you are not. I am not this, not that. I am consciousness. I am that I am, which is everything. I am that.'

∞

'There is not one way to meditate. But there is only one final pathway.'

∞

'There are no techniques to meditate. But there are different levels of attainment in meditation.'

∞

'What we desire to be happy is to stop thoughts, to let us experience our stillness.'

∞

'To meditate we need to withdraw inside to experience this one thing only.'

∞

'There are different levels of attainment in meditation we may be able to experience.'

∞

'Our level of attainment may be different at different times for each of us.'

∞

'If we find it difficult to start by withdrawing inside to see what we are and what we are not, we can turn inwards and gain some control of our mind by tethering it to one thing by following our breathing.'

∞

'Next, we can turn inwards, tethering our mind by repeating a silent sound a mantra.'

∞

'Meditation shows us we seem conditioned to keep on having thoughts instead of just being still without thoughts.'

∞

'Meditation is repeatedly stopping thoughts to let us be this inner stillness. The battle resumes every time we meditate.'

∞

'The more we meditate, the more we see thoughts are not us and so the battle of our consciousness against them becomes more effective. '

∞

'To be conscious of what we are as stillness is all we need to do. This consciousness of 'I am' is all we can be

∞

'We do not add anything to us to meditate. It is removal. We remove what is not us . . . thought. The reward is the indescribable conscious happiness of stillness.'

∞

'The method, path and goal of meditation are contained in the Biblical statement,' "Be still and know that I am God."

∞

'In other words, searching and seeing inner stillness with no thought is the method. Being conscious of 'I Am' is the only truth.'

'How do you know this?' The boy asked.

'It is what I studied and practiced my whole life. It is the art of being happy by looking within for happiness.'

'You are here as an old man, alone. Does it work?'

'Yes. But that is enough. If you want to know more I will have to tell you tomorrow. I must go and get some food.'

The old man got up and took a hessian bag with him as he walked out of the door towards the direction of the road.

When the old man had gone the boy took out a pencil and a notebook and wrote down what the man had

33

told him.

◎

The next morning the boy was once again woken by the rays of sunlight reflecting off the walls and the shiny floor.

The old man was sitting still with his eyes closed facing the hills through the window. The boy watched him and became aware that the man seemed to radiate a peacefulness which brought the boys mind to a state of being very conscious of his thoughts. It was as if the old man was showing him something and he was inviting him to follow his example.

When the old man opened his eyes from looking out the window, as he had done the day before, he turned to the boy and spoke again.

'Every morning when you sit in stillness ask, Why am I here? The answer is to be happy inside.'

'Then ask, Who am I? The answer is realised by seeing what you are not. I am not this, not that. I am consciousness. I am that I am, which is everything. I am that.'

∞

'Religions know we prefer mystery to reality.'

∞

'Maybe religion keeps you hoping there is a better place. Spirituality shows you that you are already here.'

'How do you know this?' The boy asked.

'It is what I studied and practiced my whole life. It is the art of being happy by looking within for happiness.'

'You are here as an old man, alone. Does it work?'

'Yes. But that is enough. If you want to know more I will have to tell you tomorrow. I must go and get some food.'

The old man got up and took a hessian bag with him as he walked out of the door towards the direction of the road.

When the old man had gone the boy took out a pencil and a notebook and wrote down what the man had told him.

◎

The next morning the boy was once again woken by the rays of sunlight reflecting off the walls and the shiny floor.

The old man was sitting still with his eyes closed facing the hills through the window. The boy watched him and became aware that the man seemed to radiate a peacefulness which brought the boys mind to a state of being very conscious of his thoughts. It was as if the old man was showing him something and he was inviting him to follow his example.

When the old man opened his eyes from looking out the window, as he had done the day before, he turned to the boy and spoke again.

'Every morning when you sit in stillness ask, Why am I here? The answer is to be happy inside. Then ask, Who am I? The answer is realised by seeing what you are not. I am not this, not that. I am consciousness. I am that I am, which is everything. I am that.'

∞

'Receiving kindness, even if it is just being listened

to, can restore our belief in mankind, that there are decent people.'

∞

'Even though kindness is intangible it is our most precious treasure because it can give us a purpose in life, which we can pass on.'

∞

'When kindness is not present it is time for extensive looking. Why has all the pain hit so hard that it stops kindness to our self and others?'

'How do you know this?' The boy asked.

'It is what I studied and practiced my whole life. It is the art of being happy by looking within for happiness.'

'You are here as an old man, alone. Does it work?'

'Yes. But that is enough. If you want to know more I will have to tell you tomorrow. I must go and get some food.'

The old man got up and took a hessian bag with him as he walked out of the door towards the direction of the road.

When the old man had gone the boy took out a pencil and a notebook and wrote down what the man had told him.

◎

The next morning the boy was once again woken by the rays of sunlight reflecting off the walls and the shiny floor.

The old man was sitting still with his eyes closed facing the hills through the window. The boy watched him and became aware that the man seemed to radiate a peacefulness which brought the boys mind to a state of being very conscious of his thoughts. It was as if the old man was showing him something and he was inviting him to follow his example.

When the old man opened his eyes from looking out the window, as he had done the day before, he turned to the boy and spoke again.

'Every morning when you sit in stillness ask, Why am I here? The answer is to be happy inside. Then ask, Who am I? The answer is realised by seeing what you are not. I am not this, not that. I am consciousness. I am that I am, which is everything. I am that.'

∞

'Without humility there can be no learning.'

'How do you know this?' The boy asked.

'It is what I studied and practiced my whole life. It is the art of being happy by looking within for happiness.'

'You are here as an old man, alone. Does it work?'

'Yes. But that is enough. If you want to know more I will have to tell you tomorrow. I must go and get some food.'

The old man got up and took a hessian bag with him as he walked out of the door towards the direction of the road.

When the old man had gone the boy took out a pencil and a notebook and wrote down what the man had told him.

◎

The next morning the boy was once again woken by the

rays of sunlight reflecting off the walls and the shiny floor.

The old man was sitting still with his eyes closed facing the hills through the window. The boy watched him and became aware that the man seemed to radiate a peacefulness which brought the boy's mind to a state of being very conscious of his thoughts. It was as if the old man was showing him something and he was inviting him to follow his example.

When the old man opened his eyes from looking out the window, as he had done the day before, he turned to the boy and spoke again.

'Every morning when you sit in stillness ask, Why am I here? The answer is to be happy inside. Then ask, Who am I? The answer is realised by seeing what you are not. I am not this, not that. I am consciousness. I am that I am, which is everything. I am that.'

∞

'We become so involved with thoughts; we actually see them as being us, instead of seeing them only like passing clouds in the sky.'

∞

'Detachment is separating our processes from other people's processes whilst still having a relationship.'

'How do you know this?' The boy asked.

'It is what I studied and practiced my whole life. It is the art of being happy by looking within for happiness.'

'You are here as an old man, alone. Does it work?'

'Yes. But that is enough. If you want to know more I will have to tell you tomorrow. I must go and get some food.'

The old man got up and took a hessian bag with him as he walked out of the door towards the direction of the road.

When the old man had gone the boy took out a pencil and a notebook and wrote down what the man had told him.

◎

The next morning the boy was once again woken by the rays of sunlight reflecting off the walls and the shiny floor.

The old man was sitting still with his eyes closed facing the hills through the window. The boy watched him and became aware that the man seemed to radiate a peacefulness which brought the boys mind to a state of being very conscious of his thoughts. It was as if the old man was showing him something and he was inviting him to follow his example.

When the old man opened his eyes from looking out the window, as he had done the day before, he turned to the boy and spoke again.

'Every morning when you sit in stillness ask, Why am I here? The answer is to be happy inside. Then ask, Who am I? The answer is realised by seeing what you are not. I am not this, not that. I am consciousness. I am that I am, which is everything. I am that.'

∞

'Solitude is an attitude detaching us from the distractions of the world.'

∞

'Solitude lets us detach from the distractions of the world, to experience happiness inside.'

∞

'Seeing our happiness is inside, we begin to spend more time in solitude and also with those whose view of the world is like ours.'

∞

'Being our self is none other than being conscious of the happiness of stillness inside.'

'How do you know this?' The boy asked.

'It is what I studied and practiced my whole life. It is the art of being happy by looking within for happiness.'

'You are here as an old man, alone. Does it work?'

'Yes. But that is enough. If you want to know more I will have to tell you tomorrow. I must go and get some food.'

The old man got up and took a hessian bag with him as he walked out of the door towards the direction of the road.

When the old man had gone the boy took out a pencil and a notebook and wrote down what the man had told him.

◎

The next morning the boy was once again woken by the rays of sunlight reflecting off the walls and the shiny floor.

The old man was sitting still with his eyes closed facing the hills through the window. The boy watched him and became aware that the man seemed to radiate a peacefulness which brought the boys mind to a state of being very conscious of his thoughts. It was as if the old man was showing him something and he was inviting him to follow his example.

When the old man opened his eyes from looking out the window, as he had done the day before, he turned to the boy and spoke again.

'Every morning when you sit in stillness ask, Why am I here? The answer is to be happy inside. Then ask, Who am I? The answer is realised by seeing what you are not. I am not this, not that. I am consciousness. I am that I am, which is everything. I am that.'

∞

'Silence is the language of stillness.

∞

'Consciousness of inner stillness, happiness and truth are perhaps only words for the same thing.'

∞

'There are no words for consciousness of stillness.'
'How do you know this?' The boy asked.
'It is what I studied and practiced my whole life. It is the art of being happy by looking within for happiness.'
'You are here as an old man, alone. Does it work?'
'Yes. But that is enough. If you want to know more I will have to tell you tomorrow. I must go and get some food.'

The old man got up and took a hessian bag with him as he walked out of the door towards the direction of

41

the road.

When the old man had gone the boy took out a pencil and a notebook and wrote down what the man had told him.

◎

The next morning the boy was once again woken by the rays of sunlight reflecting off the walls and the shiny floor.

The old man was sitting still with his eyes closed facing the hills through the window. The boy watched him and became aware that the man seemed to radiate a peacefulness which brought the boys mind to a state of being very conscious of his thoughts. It was as if the old man was showing him something and he was inviting him to follow his example.

When the old man opened his eyes from looking out the window, as he had done the day before, he turned to the boy and spoke again.

'Every morning when you sit in stillness ask, Why am I here? The answer is to be happy inside. Then ask, Who am I? The answer is realised by seeing what you are not. I am not this, not that. I am consciousness. I am that I am, which is everything. I am that.'

∞

'These are the two questions which you should ask every day at the beginning of your day.' There was a pause almost as if he wanted the boy to remember.

∞

'The answer to Why am I here is this. It is to find

the happiness which is inside you.' He paused again, once more so as if that the boy could remember what he had said.

∞

'The answer to the Who am I is this. You find out by finding out what you are not. You say you are not this and not that. You are not your thoughts. You are not a collection of thoughts which is called the ego.' He paused again as if to let the boy absorb what he had said.

∞

'What is really you is not your body. It is not your memories or your thoughts about the future. You are simply consciousness without thoughts.' He paused again.

∞

'What has always been there aware of all your thoughts is your consciousness. It is what sees without eyes, what hears without ears. That is what you are.' There was one last pause, the longest.

∞

'Seeing that you are this consciousness of everything which is the same as the consciousness of the universe is what we are. You must actually be it.

'How do you know this?' The boy asked.

'It is what I studied and practiced my whole life. It is the art of being happy by looking within for happiness.'

'You are here as an old man, alone. Does it work?'

'Yes. But that is enough. If you want to know more I will have to tell you tomorrow. I must go and get some food.'

The old man got up and took a hessian bag with him as he walked out of the door towards the direction of the road. He did not return.

When the old man had gone the boy took out a pencil and a notebook and wrote down what the man had told him.

Later he thought he heard a sound outside. He went out to see what it was with his oil lamp as it was dark.

He noticed a young man who had put his bag against a tree. He was sitting in a deep sleep.

He held the lamp up to look at the young man's face. When he held the lamp up, he noticed the skin of his own hands had skin creases of an old man.

∞

2.

SAGES

Like Groundhog Day, it can seem that repeated effort keeps on returning us to the same place. But with perseverance, eventually we see who we are.

The young woman woke and saw the poor light of the pre-dawn darkness. She turned and acknowledged the light again then she slipped out of bed.

She bathed then dressed and went to revive the embers of the fire from the previous night's cooking. She added small dry twigs, then small branches then laid three logs on the smoking logs.

After a breakfast of bread and milk the young woman tidied and cleaned the two small rooms. She then began to make bread. Whilst kneading the bread she went outside to see what the day was like. She felt the cool air on her face and arms because clouds were still hiding the heat and light from the sun. She knew the heat of the day would slowly appear after two hours and after that, three people would arrive to collect loaves of bread for their day.

When the sun had set the young woman began to make the second batch of bread. Whilst kneading the bread she went outside to see what the day was like. She felt the warm air on her face and arms because of the heat still rising from the hot earth. She knew the cooler night air would slowly appear after two hours and after that, three people would arrive to collect loaves of bread for the next day.

When they had gone, she ate the bread she had made along with the vegetables and milk she had exchanged for loaves of bread. As the fire died down she fell asleep.

◎

The young woman woke and saw the poor light of the pre-dawn darkness. She turned and acknowledged the light again then she slipped out of bed.

She bathed then dressed and went to revive the embers of the fire from the previous night's cooking. She added small dry twigs, then small branches then laid three logs on the smoking logs.

After a breakfast of bread and milk the young woman tidied and cleaned the two small rooms. She then began to make bread. Whilst kneading the bread she went outside to see what the day was like. She felt the cool air on her face and arms because clouds were still hiding the heat and light from the sun. She knew the heat of the day would slowly appear after two hours and after that, three people would arrive to collect loaves of bread for their day

Whilst kneading the bread the young woman thought she heard a voice singing. She thought she had imagined it as no one came to this area of the land near the coast as it led to nowhere. But there is it was again. She thought she heard a young woman's voice talking or maybe even singing. She went outside and looked around but there was no one.

When the sun had set the young woman began to make the second batch of bread. Whilst kneading the bread she went outside to see what the day was like. She felt the warm air on her face and arms because of the heat still rising from the hot earth. She knew the cooler night air would slowly appear after two hours and after that, three people would arrive to collect loaves of bread for the next day.

When they had gone, she ate the bread she had made along with the vegetables and milk she had exchanged for loaves of bread. As the fire died down she fell asleep.

◎

The young woman woke and saw the poor light of the pre-dawn darkness. She turned and acknowledged the light again then she slipped out of bed.

She bathed then dressed and went to revive the embers of the fire from the previous night's cooking. She added small dry twigs, then small branches then laid three logs on the smoking logs.

After a breakfast of bread and milk the young woman tidied and cleaned the two small rooms. She then began to make bread. Whilst kneading the bread she went outside to see what the day was like. She felt the cool air on her face and arms because clouds were still hiding the heat and light from the sun. She knew the heat of the day would slowly appear after two hours and after that, three people would arrive to collect loaves of bread for their day.

Whilst kneading the bread the young woman thought she heard a voice singing. She thought she had imagined it as no one came to this area of the land near the coast as it led to nowhere. But there is it was again. She thought she heard a young woman's voice talking or maybe even singing. She went outside and looked around but there was no one.

She remembered this happened the day before at exactly the same time. There were no visitors to the area and certainly none she knew of. She could not work out where the young woman's voice was coming from or what it was that maybe sounded like a young woman's voice singing.

When the sun had set the young woman began to make the second batch of bread.

Whilst kneading the bread she went outside to see what the day was like. She felt the warm air on her face and arms because of the heat still rising from the hot earth. She knew the cooler night air would slowly appear after two hours and after that, three people would arrive to collect loaves of bread for the next day.

When they had gone, she ate the bread she had made

49

along with the vegetables and milk she had exchanged for loaves of bread. As the fire died down she fell asleep.

The young woman woke and saw the poor light of the pre-dawn darkness. She turned and acknowledged the light again then she slipped out of bed.

She bathed then dressed and went to revive the embers of the fire from the previous night's cooking. She added small dry twigs, then small branches then laid three logs on the smoking logs.

After a breakfast of bread and milk the young woman tidied and cleaned the two small rooms. She then began to make bread. Whilst kneading the bread she went outside to see what the day was like. She felt the cool air on her face and arms because clouds were still hiding the heat and light from the sun. She knew the heat of the day would slowly appear after two hours and after that, three people would arrive to collect loaves of bread for their day.

Whilst kneading the bread the young woman thought she heard a voice singing. She thought she had imagined it as no one came to this area of the land near the coast as it led to nowhere. But there is it was again. She thought she heard a young woman's voice talking or maybe even singing. She went outside and looked around but there was no one.

She remembered this happened the day before at exactly the same time. There were no visitors to the area and certainly none she knew of. She could not work out where the young woman's voice was coming from or what it was that maybe sounded like a young woman's voice.

She went back to kneading the bread and this time the voice was louder. It was closer. It was in the room with

50

her. She had begun singing. She immediately stopped. She did not usually sing.

When the sun had set the young woman began to make the second batch of bread. Whilst kneading the bread she went outside to see what the day was like. She felt the warm air on her face and arms because of the heat still rising from the hot earth. She knew the cooler night air would slowly appear after two hours and after that, three people would arrive to collect loaves of bread for the next day.

When they had gone, she ate the bread she had made along with the vegetables and milk she had exchanged for loaves of bread. As the fire died down she fell asleep.

◎

The young woman woke and saw the poor light of the pre-dawn darkness. She turned and acknowledged the light again then she slipped out of bed.

She bathed then dressed and went to revive the embers of the fire from the previous night's cooking. She added small dry twigs, then small branches then laid three logs on the smoking logs.

After a breakfast of bread and milk the young woman tidied and cleaned the two small rooms. She then began to make bread. Whilst kneading the bread she went outside to see what the day was like. She felt the cool air on her face and arms because clouds were still hiding the heat and light from the sun. She knew the heat of the day would slowly appear after two hours and after that, three people would arrive to collect loaves of bread for their day.

Whilst kneading the bread the young woman thought she heard a voice singing. She thought she had imagined it as no one came to this area of the land near

51

the coast as it led to nowhere. But there is it was again. She thought she heard a young woman's voice talking or maybe even singing. She went outside and looked around but there was no one.

She remembered this happened the day before at exactly the same time. There were no visitors to the area and certainly none she knew of. She could not work out where the young woman's voice was coming from or what it was that maybe sounded like a young woman's voice.

She went back to kneading the bread and this time the voice was louder. It was closer. It was in the room with her. She had begun singing. She immediately stopped. She did not usually sing. But now, even though she stopped she could hear a voice singing. She felt very strange as if she was about to become ill so she went to lay down on the bed.

When the sun had set the young woman began to make the second batch of bread.

Whilst kneading the bread she went outside to see what the day was like. She felt the warm air on her face and arms because of the heat still rising from the hot earth. She knew the cooler night air would slowly appear after two hours and after that, three people would arrive to collect loaves of bread for the next day.

When they had gone, she ate the bread she had made along with the vegetables and milk she had exchanged for loaves of bread. As the fire died down she fell asleep.

◎

The young woman woke and saw the poor light of the pre-dawn darkness. She turned and acknowledged the light again then she slipped out of bed.

She bathed then dressed and went to revive the

embers of the fire from the previous night's cooking. She added small dry twigs, then small branches then laid three logs on the smoking logs.

After a breakfast of bread and milk the young woman tidied and cleaned the two small rooms. She then began to make bread. Whilst kneading the bread she went outside to see what the day was like. She felt the cool air on her face and arms because clouds were still hiding the heat and light from the sun. She knew the heat of the day would slowly appear after two hours and after that, three people would arrive to collect loaves of bread for their day.

Whilst kneading the bread the young woman thought she heard a voice singing. She thought she had imagined it as no one came to this area of the land near the coast as it led to nowhere. But there is it was again. She thought she heard a young woman's voice talking or maybe even singing. She went outside and looked around but there was no one.

She remembered this happened the day before at exactly the same time. There were no visitors to the area and certainly none she knew of. She could not work out where the young woman's voice was coming from or what it was that maybe sounded like a young woman's voice.

She went back to kneading the bread and this time the voice was louder. It was closer. It was in the room with her. She had begun singing. She immediately stopped. She did not usually sing. But now, even though she stopped she could hear a voice singing. She felt very strange as if she was about to become ill so she went to lay down on the bed.

The young woman was woken by knocking on the wooden door. She listened and there it was again. She got off the bed and gathered and smoothed out her clothes as she never had visitors. Nervously and fully prepared to defend her small dwelling against any intruder she opened the door.

At first she couldn't see the face of the figure who was silhouetted by light from the rising sun behind. The young woman saw that it was the figure of an older woman and then made out the face which had a gentle smile. She noticed immediately that the woman's smile was serene, unlike how she saw her own smile.

She beckoned her inside but the woman did not come in. Instead, she stood on the threshold of the dwelling.

'I am looking for a room for a night or two.'

'I don't have a spare room, just the floor of the kitchen. But I can make up a mattress and I have extra blankets and pillows.'

'This is kind as you don't even know me.

'What's your business here?'

'I am travelling to meet my sister in the south.'

'Then you are welcome to stay. I can make a bed for you.'

'This is kind of you.'

'This morning I have made some warm bread and there is some milk if you are thirsty.'

'This is kindness again.' The woman said, putting her shoulder bag on the stone floor.

The sun was setting and they got up to go inside the dwelling. When the sun had set the woman began to make the second batch of bread.

Whilst kneading the bread she went outside to see what the day was like. She felt the warm air on her face and arms because of the heat still rising from the hot earth. She knew the cooler night air would slowly appear after two hours and after that, three people would arrive to collect loaves of bread for the next day.

When they had gone, the young woman sat with her as they ate the bread she had made along with the vegetables and milk she had exchanged for loaves of bread. As the fire died down they fell asleep in their beds.

◎

The young woman woke and saw the poor light of the pre-dawn darkness. She turned and acknowledged the light again then she slipped out of bed.

She bathed then dressed and went to revive the embers of the fire from the previous night's cooking. She added small dry twigs, then small branches then laid three logs on the smoking logs.

Beside the makeshift bed lay with the woman's large shoulder bag. She thought she may have gone for a walk in the early morning cool air so she once again she waited for her to return.

After a breakfast of bread and milk the young woman tidied and cleaned the two small rooms. She then began to make bread. Whilst kneading the bread she went outside to see what the day was like. She felt the cool air on her face and arms because clouds were still hiding the heat and light from the sun. She knew the heat of the day would slowly appear after two hours and after that, three people would arrive to collect loaves of bread for their day.

Whilst kneading the bread the young woman thought she heard a voice singing, just like the last few days. It was the same voice, the one she had heard before. But now it was not her singing. It was coming from outside the house. It was as if she was being called by someone outside.

She went outside and looked around but there was

no one. Then she heard the voice singing again. It was coming from the back of the dwelling. She walked around and there sitting on one of several logs, looking into the distance was the woman. She was not singing and it was then that she realised that her own inner voice was calling her to see this woman.

The woman sat still with her eyes closed as the young woman came and sat opposite her.

She saw that the woman's face looked more serene than the day before when she had first met her. The young woman had a sense that the calmness and peace in the woman's face was very pure. She could only liken her serene state to the innocence of a flower or the face of a child.

She sat down opposite her and looked at her. As she did, she noticed her thoughts slowed down so much that there was only the occasional thought.

She was sitting being still with this woman and not thinking as much as usual. Several times she would suddenly be aware that she had been in a state she could not describe but which was very pleasant. It was neither sleep nor being in a trance, but it was so relaxed she wanted more of it. She felt she didn't want the woman to open her eyes. She felt she didn't want her to leave and go on her journey more south.

'Can you tell me how I can get happiness like you?'

'Happiness is not a Possession. What makes you think you don't have happiness?'

'I've lived here since my aunt died. She brought me up. I feel detached and not like everyone else. I am very serious about everything and everyone but I just can't seem to find happiness in myself like everyone else.'

'What makes you so sure they are happy?'

'I'm not sure, but they seem happier than me.'

'What you see on the outside is rarely what is going on in the inside because few know that our happiness is inside and even fewer know how to look inside to find it.'

'How do I look inside?'

'Knowing your self is a skill learnt like any other skill.' But is the most important one of your whole life.'

'How do I learn that skill?'

'If you are hungry enough, like a starving person, you can learn it.'

The sun was setting and so they got up to go inside the dwelling. When the sun had set the young woman began to make the second batch of bread.

Whilst kneading the bread she went outside to see what the day was like. She felt the warm air on her face and arms because of the heat still rising from the hot earth. She knew the cooler night air would slowly appear after two hours and after that, three people would arrive to collect loaves of bread for the next day.

When they had gone, the woman sat with her as they ate the bread she had made along with the vegetables and milk she had exchanged for loaves of bread. As the fire died down they fell asleep in their beds.

◎

The young woman woke and saw the poor light of the pre-dawn darkness. She turned and acknowledged the light again then she slipped out of bed.

She bathed then dressed and went to revive the embers of the fire from the previous night's cooking. She added small dry twigs, then small branches then laid three logs on the smoking logs.

Beside the makeshift bed lay with the woman's

large shoulder bag. She thought she may have gone for a walk in the early morning cool air so she waited for her to return.

After a breakfast of bread and milk the young woman tidied and cleaned the two small rooms. She then began to make bread. Whilst kneading the bread she went outside to see what the day was like. She felt the cool air on her face and arms because clouds were still hiding the heat and light from the sun. She knew the heat of the day would slowly appear after two hours and after that, three people would arrive to collect loaves of bread for their day.

Whilst kneading the bread the young woman thought she heard a voice singing, just like the last few days. It was the same voice, the one she had heard before. But it was not her singing. It was coming from outside the house. It was as if she was being called by someone outside. She went outside and looked around but there was no one.

Then she heard the voice singing again. It was coming from the back of the dwelling. She walked around and there sitting on one of several logs, looking into the distance was the woman. She was not singing and it was then that she again realised that her own inner voice was calling her to see this woman.

The woman sat still with her eyes closed as the young woman came and sat opposite her.

She saw that the woman's face looked more serene than the day before when she had first met her. The young woman had a sense that the calmness and peace in the woman's face was very pure. She could only liken her serene state to the innocence of a flower or the face of a child.

She sat down opposite her and looked at her. As she did, she noticed her thoughts slowed down so much that there was only the occasional thought.

She was sitting being still with this woman and not thinking as much as usual.

Several times she would suddenly be aware that she had been in a state she could not describe but which was very pleasant. It was neither sleep nor being in a trance, but it was so relaxed she wanted more of it. She felt she didn't want the woman to open her eyes. She felt she didn't want her to leave and go on her journey more south.

'Can you tell me how I can get happiness like you?'

'As we saw yesterday, happiness is not a Possession. You may have looked at acquiring money, things, power, influence or knowledge to make you happy. You may have looked at having all of these possessions to make you happy. But these will make you bored and you will endlessly keep going onto the next best thing.'

∞

'Possessions lead to fear of their use and loss. Fear and loss make us think we will be happier if we can more securely possess them, so an endless pursuit begins. Loss anxiety makes us try harder to possess what does not even make us happy.'

∞

'Don't be misled by beauty because Beauty is something recognised outside, happiness is always inside. Beauty is derived from the senses, happiness is revealed inside. Beauty is a synthesis of fine thinking, happiness is simply being in the heart with no thoughts.'

∞

'There is no relationship between any form of possession and happiness. How do we know this? A powerful wealthy influential person will always have loss anxiety about their securities. They cannot be as happy as the person who has found happiness inside. Seeing that acquiring things, money, power, influence or knowledge does not make you happy, there is only one place left to look for happiness. Inside.'

The sun was setting and they got up to go inside the dwelling. When the sun had set the young woman began to make the second batch of bread.

Whilst kneading the bread she went outside to see what the day was like. She felt the warm air on her face and arms because of the heat still rising from the hot earth. She knew the cooler night air would slowly appear after two hours and after that, three people would arrive to collect loaves of bread for the next day.

When they had gone, the woman sat with her as they ate the bread she had made along with the vegetables and milk she had exchanged for loaves of bread. As the fire died down they fell asleep in their beds.

◎

The young woman woke and saw the poor light of the pre-dawn darkness. She turned and acknowledged the light again then she slipped out of bed.

She bathed then dressed and went to revive the embers of the fire from the previous night's cooking. She added small dry twigs, then small branches then laid three logs on the smoking logs.

After a breakfast of bread and milk the young

woman tidied and cleaned the two small rooms. She then began to make bread. Whilst kneading the bread she went outside to see what the day was like. She felt the cool air on her face and arms because clouds were still hiding the heat and light from the sun. She knew the heat of the day would slowly appear after two hours and after that, three people would arrive to collect loaves of bread for their day.

After the three people had collected their loaves the young woman went around to the back of the house where the woman was sitting the day before. The woman was sitting still with her eyes closed as the young woman came and sat opposite her.

She saw once again that the woman's face looked more serene than when she had first met her. The young woman had a sense that the calmness and peace in the woman's face was very pure. Again, she could only liken her serene state to the innocence of a flower or the face of a child.

Sitting down opposite her and looking at her, she noticed her thoughts slowed down so much that there was only the occasional thought. She was sitting being still with this woman and not thinking as much as usual.

Several times she would suddenly be aware that she had been in state she could not describe but which was very pleasant. It was neither sleep nor being in a trance, but it was so relaxed she wanted more of it.

She felt she didn't want the woman to open her eyes. She felt she didn't want her to leave and go on her journey more south. She too closed her eyes.

Some time after she opened her eyes, she saw the woman also open her eyes and was not at all surprised to see the young woman sitting opposite her.

'What else can you say about happiness?' The young woman asked.

'To be happy you need to see you can't acquire it by adding something to yourself. Instead, see that you have to remove something about you. Get rid of your belief that you can acquire happiness by seeing you already have it.'

∞

'Happiness is seen by getting rid of searching for happiness because it is already inside you.'

∞

'Happiness is seen by getting rid of looking outside of you for happiness.'

∞

'Happiness is seen by getting rid of thinking security of any kind will make you happy.'

∞

'Happiness is seen by constant effort to be happy.'

The sun was setting and they got up to go inside the dwelling. When the sun had set the young woman began to make the second batch of bread.

Whilst kneading the bread she went outside to see what the day was like. She felt the warm air on her face and arms because of the heat still rising from the hot earth. She knew the cooler night air would slowly appear after two hours and after that, three people would arrive to collect loaves of bread for the next day.

When they had gone, the woman sat with her as

they ate the bread she had made along with the vegetables and milk she had exchanged for loaves of bread. As the fire died down they fell asleep in their beds.

◎

The young woman woke and saw the poor light of the pre-dawn darkness. She turned and acknowledged the light again then she slipped out of bed.

She bathed then dressed and went to revive the embers of the fire from the previous night's cooking. She added small dry twigs, then small branches then laid three logs on the smoking logs.

After a breakfast of bread and milk the young woman tidied and cleaned the two small rooms. She then began to make bread. Whilst kneading the bread she went outside to see what the day was like. She felt the cool air on her face and arms because clouds were still hiding the heat and light from the sun. She knew the heat of the day would slowly appear after two hours and after that, three people would arrive to collect loaves of bread for their day.

After the three people had collected their loaves the young woman went around to the back of the house where the woman was sitting the day before. The woman was sitting still with her eyes closed as the young woman came and sat opposite her.

She saw once again that the woman's face looked more serene than when she had first met her. The young woman had a sense that the calmness and peace in the woman's face was very pure. Again, she could only liken her serene state to the innocence of a flower or the face of a child.

Sitting down opposite her and looking at her, she noticed her thoughts slowed down so much that there was only the occasional thought. She was sitting being still with this woman and not thinking as much as usual.

Several times she would suddenly be aware that she had been in state she could not describe but which was very pleasant. It was neither sleep nor being in a trance, but it was so relaxed she wanted more of it.

She felt she didn't want the woman to open her eyes. She felt she didn't want her to leave and go on her journey more south. She too closed her eyes.

Some time after she opened her eyes, she saw the woman also open her eyes and was not at all surprised to see the young woman sitting opposite her.

'Why is it so difficult to be happy?' The young woman asked.

'There are three things we don't see. The first is that to access happiness we have to get rid of thinking it is outside. Like light is always here from the sun but we may be busy looking at something else; we only need to turn inside to see our happiness.'

∞

'We may not be able to be happy all the time but our happiness is always here inside us. Your happiness depends on seeing your happiness is already inside you and is not something new which can be acquired from outside.'

∞

'The second is that you can't actually ever be happy tomorrow, only today. You can only be happy today, in the present, right now, so give up the search in the future, so you can see it now. Happiness is inside and we can only be happy right now today.

∞

'The third is that to be happy now, you have to be happy with what you have and have no want. To be happy with what you are and what you have is to be happy with just sufficient. Sufficient is what is enough. Enough for how long? Well today is how long.'

The sun was setting and they got up to go inside the dwelling. When the sun had set the young woman began to make the second batch of bread.

Whilst kneading the bread she went outside to see what the day was like. She felt the warm air on her face and arms because of the heat still rising from the hot earth. She knew the cooler night air would slowly appear after two hours and after that, three people would arrive to collect loaves of bread for the next day.

When they had gone, the woman sat with her as they ate the bread she had made along with the vegetables and milk she had exchanged for loaves of bread. As the fire died down they fell asleep in their beds.

◎

The young woman woke and saw the poor light of the pre-dawn darkness. She turned and acknowledged the light again then she slipped out of bed.

She bathed then dressed and went to revive the embers of the fire from the previous night's cooking. She added small dry twigs, then small branches then laid three logs on the smoking logs.

Beside the makeshift bed lay with the woman's

65

large shoulder bag. She thought she was probably sitting again outside at the back of the dwelling.

After a breakfast of bread and milk the young woman tidied and cleaned the two small rooms. She then began to make bread. Whilst kneading the bread she went outside to see what the day was like. She felt the cool air on her face and arms because clouds were still hiding the heat and light from the sun. She knew the heat of the day would slowly appear after two hours and after that, three people would arrive to collect loaves of bread for their day.

After the young woman had tidied and cleaned the two small rooms she began to make some bread. Whilst kneading the bread the young woman thought she heard a voice singing, just like the last few days. It was the same voice, the one she had heard before. But now, once more, it was not her singing. It was coming from outside the house.

She went outside and looked around but there was no one. Then she heard the voice singing again. Once again it was coming from the back of the dwelling. She walked around and there sitting on one of several logs looking into the distance was the woman.

The woman sat still with her eyes closed as the young woman came and sat opposite her.

She saw once again that the woman's face looked more serene than when she had first met her. The young woman had a sense that the calmness and peace in the woman's face was very pure. She could only liken her serene state to the innocence of a flower or the face of a child.

She sat down opposite her and looked at her. As she did, she noticed her thoughts slowed down so much that there was only the occasional thought.

She was sitting being still with this woman and not thinking as much as usual. Several times she would suddenly be aware that she had been in state she could not describe but which was very pleasant. It was neither sleep nor being in a trance, but it was so relaxed she wanted more of it. She felt she didn't want the woman to open her eyes. She felt she didn't want her to leave and go on her journey more south.

Then as if in slow motion the woman opened her eyes and was not at all surprised to see the young woman sitting opposite her.

'When can I be happy like you?

'When you see you are as happy as you can be today without wanting anything, you have found happiness.'

∞

'When you are free from pain and free from desiring pleasure, you are happy. Possessions lead to fear of their use and loss.'

∞

'When you see this you see you have no want.'

∞

'When you see you have no want you cannot be happier.'

∞

'With no want you are happy'

∞

'Do you know a person with no want?'

∞

'The easiest way to make yourself an exile from your happiness is to start thinking about the past or what you want in the future.'

The sun was setting and they got up to go inside the dwelling. When the sun had set the young woman began to make the second batch of bread.

Whilst kneading the bread she went outside to see what the day was like. She felt the warm air on her face and arms because of the heat still rising from the hot earth. She knew the cooler night air would slowly appear after two hours and after that, three people would arrive to collect loaves of bread for the next day.

When they had gone, the woman sat with her as they ate the bread she had made along with the vegetables and milk she had exchanged for loaves of bread. As the fire died down they fell asleep in their beds.

◎

The young woman woke and saw the poor light of the pre-dawn darkness. She turned and acknowledged the light again then she slipped out of bed.

She bathed then dressed and went to revive the embers of the fire from the previous night's cooking. She added small dry twigs, then small branches then laid three logs on the smoking logs.

After a breakfast of bread and milk the young woman tidied and cleaned the two small rooms. She then began to make bread. Whilst kneading the bread she went

68

outside to see what the day was like. She felt the cool air on her face and arms because clouds were still hiding the heat and light from the sun. She knew the heat of the day would slowly appear after two hours and after that, three people would arrive to collect loaves of bread for their day.

After the three people had collected their loaves the young woman went around to the back of the house where the woman was sitting the day before.

The woman was sitting still with her eyes closed as the young woman came and sat opposite her.

She saw once again that the woman's face looked more serene than when she had first met her. The young woman had a sense that the calmness and peace in the woman's face was very pure. Again, she could only liken her serene state to the innocence of a flower or the face of a child.

Sitting down opposite her and looking at her, she noticed her thoughts slowed down so much that there was only the occasional thought. She was sitting being still with this woman and not thinking as much as usual.

Several times she would suddenly be aware that she had been in state she could not describe but which was very pleasant. It was neither sleep nor being in a trance, but it was so relaxed she wanted more of it. She felt she didn't want the woman to open her eyes. She felt she didn't want her to leave and go on her journey more south. She too closed her eyes.

Then as if in slow motion the woman opened her eyes and was not at all surprised to see the young woman sitting opposite her.

'How come you are so happy?'

'We are not born unhappy but our circumstances make us unhappy, so we try to find the happiness we know is inside. This is our nature. But we make the mistake of looking for happiness outside rather than inside.'

'Why do we look outside rather than inside?'

'People and organisations are more interested in you not looking inside. They want you to depend on them for your happiness.'

∞

'Our happiness is our self which is the same as everything in the Universe and no different from it.'

∞

'Religions point to seeing our inner self as our higher power inside us or as God. Most simply this is consciousness of 'I am.' This can be seen in the words from the east and the west over the last three thousand years.'

∞

'Let us demystify religions.'

∞

'What is really you is not your body. It is not your memories or your thoughts about the future. You are simply consciousness without thoughts.'

∞

'What has always been there aware of all your thoughts is your consciousness. It is what sees without eyes, what hears without ears. That is what you are.' There was one last pause, the longest.

∞

'Seeing that you are this consciousness, it has to be the same as all consciousness. This has to be the consciousness of everything, which is the same as the consciousness of the universe. You eventually see this is in truth what you are. But you must actually be it.'

∞

'We ask what the mystery of life is. Why are we here? What are we here for? The answer is simple. We are only here to be happy.'

∞

'Religions know we prefer mystery to reality. The ancients knew it.'

∞

'The ancient civilisations knew it. They knew that happiness was inside. In Judaism, when Moses asked God for his name he answered, "I Am That I Am. Thus shalt you say unto the children of Israel, I Am has sent me to you." Jehovah means I am. So knowing the self, God is known as they are taken to be the same.'

∞

'The Pashupati Seal is a soapstone seal discovered in the Indus Valley Civilisation. It is estimated to have been carved around 2350 BC and is thought to be the earliest prototype of the God Shiva. The seal shows a seated cross-legged figure in the yogic lotus meditation posture with arms pointing downwards. It is important because it is one of the first communications from our ancient ancestors which reflects the stillness of silently looking inwards.'

∞

'In Hinduism the mind is helped to look inwards by, "Netti Netti," from the Brihadaranyaka Upanishad written around 800 BC, meaning, "Neither this neither this," which helps the mind to constantly disidentify with anything other than that which is everything.'

∞

'One of the ancient Greek's key instructions, "Know the self," was written on the portals of their most important temple, the Temple of Apollo in Delphi.'

∞

'In the Hebrew Bible or the Tanaka, in Psalm 46, God is assumed to be inside, "Be still and know that I am God."

∞

'And again in Christianity in Luke 17, it says, "The kingdom of God is within you." Do you see it?'

∞

'Even Shakespeare pointed man strongly inside, "This above all-to thine own self be true."

∞

'In the 8th century, an Indian guru, Adi Shankara, said, "The fool takes the reflection of the sun in the water of a pot to be the sun; the wise man eliminates pot, water, and reflection and knows the sun in the sky as it really is, single and unaffected, but illuminating all three. In the same way the fool through error and misperception, identifies himself with the ego and its reflected light experienced through the medium of the intellect. The wise and discriminating man eliminates body, intellect, and reflected light of consciousness and probes deeply into his real Self which illuminates all three while remaining uniform in the ether of the heart. Thereby he realises the eternal witness which is absolute knowledge, illuminating all three."

∞

'All of this was most clearly summarised by another Indian Guru, Ramana Maharshi when he said in 1937, "Your duty is to be and not to be this or that. I AM that I AM, sums up the whole truth. The method is summarised in, Be still. What does stillness mean? It means, destroy yourself. Because any form or shape is the cause of trouble. Give up the notion that "I am so and so."

∞

'So you see, they all say that happiness is inside. We have to be that consciousness not just in the morning when

73

we sit still. But gradually we become that consciousness 'I Am' more and more throughout the day. We surrender to it. We surrender our Self to the Universe. Then we become it.'

The sun was setting and they got up to go inside the dwelling. When the sun had set the young woman began to make the second batch of bread.

Whilst kneading the bread she went outside to see what the day was like. She felt the warm air on her face and arms because of the heat still rising from the hot earth. She knew the cooler night air would slowly appear after two hours and after that, three people would arrive to collect loaves of bread for the next day.

When they had gone, the woman sat with her as they ate the bread she had made along with the vegetables and milk she had exchanged for loaves of bread. As the fire died down they fell asleep in their beds.

◎

The young woman woke and saw the poor light of the pre-dawn darkness. She turned and acknowledged the light again then she slipped out of bed.

She bathed then dressed and went to revive the embers of the fire from the previous night's cooking. She added small dry twigs, then small branches then laid three logs on the smoking logs.

After a breakfast of bread and milk the young woman tidied and cleaned the two small rooms. She then began to make bread. Whilst kneading the bread she went outside to see what the day was like. She felt the cool air on her face and arms because clouds were still hiding the heat and light from the sun. She knew the heat of the day would slowly appear after two hours and after that, three people would arrive to collect loaves of bread for their day.

After the three people had collected their loaves the young woman went around to the back of the house where the woman was sitting the day before.

The woman was sitting still with her eyes closed as the young woman came and sat opposite her.

She saw once again that the woman's face looked more serene than when she had first met her. The young woman had a sense that the calmness and peace in the woman's face was very pure. Again she could only liken her serene state to the innocence of a flower or the face of a child.

Sitting down opposite her and looking at her, she noticed her thoughts slowed down so much that there was only the occasional thought. She was sitting being still with this woman and not thinking as much as usual.

Several times she would suddenly be aware that she had been in state she could not describe but which was very pleasant. It was neither sleep nor being in a trance, but it was so relaxed she wanted more of it. She felt she didn't want the woman to open her eyes. She felt she didn't want her to leave and go on her journey more south. She too closed her eyes.

Some time after she opened her eyes, she saw the woman also open her eyes and was not at all surprised to see the young woman sitting opposite her.

'What is the meaning of our life? Asked the young woman.

'This is reality for me.' Said the woman. 'Sitting in stillness in happiness inside.

'I'm not sure I get that.'

'Do you know who you really are?'

'I'm just me, a simple householder.'

'You are not just a simple householder.'

'By seeing what we are not we see who we really are.'

'The world which we believe is real, is only the one we experience with all our senses in our body. It is what we believe is real after we have processed all the information with our thoughts in our brain.'

'I don't understand.'

'Although we believe that the world we experience is reality, we have just fooled ourselves with our thinking. When you close your eyes and let your inner self just be without thoughts, you see that thoughts keep on coming and going. It is then you see you can look down on thoughts, like looking from high up on a mountain down onto a river below.'

The sun was setting and they got up to go inside the dwelling. When the sun had set the young woman began to make the second batch of bread.

Whilst kneading the bread she went outside to see what the day was like. She felt the warm air on her face and arms because of the heat still rising from the hot earth. She knew the cooler night air would slowly appear after two hours and after that, three people would arrive to collect loaves of bread for the next day.

When they had gone, the woman sat with her as they ate the bread she had made along with the vegetables and milk she had exchanged for loaves of bread. As the fire died down they fell asleep in their beds.

◎

The young woman woke and saw the poor light of the pre-dawn darkness. She turned and acknowledged the light again then she slipped out of bed.

She bathed then dressed and went to revive the embers of the fire from the previous night's cooking. She added small dry twigs, then small branches then laid three logs on the smoking logs.

After a breakfast of bread and milk the young woman tidied and cleaned the two small rooms. She then began to make bread. Whilst kneading the bread she went outside to see what the day was like. She felt the cool air on her face and arms because clouds were still hiding the heat and light from the sun. She knew the heat of the day would slowly appear after two hours and after that, three people would arrive to collect loaves of bread for their day.

After the three people had collected their loaves the young woman went around to the back of the house where the woman was sitting the day before.

The woman was sitting still with her eyes closed as the young woman came and sat opposite her.

She saw once again that the woman's face looked more serene than when she had first met her. The young woman had a sense that the calmness and peace in the woman's face was very pure. Again, she could only liken her serene state to the innocence of a flower or the face of a child.

Sitting down opposite her and looking at her, she noticed her thoughts slowed down so much that there was only the occasional thought. She was sitting being still with this woman and not thinking as much as usual.

Several times she would suddenly be aware that she had been in state she could not describe but which was very pleasant. It was neither sleep nor being in a trance, but it was so relaxed she wanted more of it. She felt she didn't want the woman to open her eyes. She felt she didn't want her to leave and go on her journey more south. She too closed her eyes.

Some time after she opened her eyes, she saw the woman also open her eyes and was not at all surprised to see the young woman sitting opposite her.

'I looked at what you said yesterday about me being consciousness and not just being my thoughts.'

'Seeing our goal is inner stillness, we try to use thinking to find it but we can only find our stillness by being still, not by thinking about it.'

∞

'When we look inside at 'Who are we?' we become conscious we are not thought.'

∞

'It is a surprise to discover that you are not your thoughts, which through reflection seem like imposters.'

∞

'We are taught and programmed to believe we are a bundle of thoughts called the ego.'

∞

'But in meditation you see you are not just a bundle of thoughts.'

∞

'When you stay with this, you begin to see consciousness comes before thought. Consciousness is always here. Thought comes and goes.'

∞

'In meditation you see you are consciousness which is not a thought but is what creates thought. This is what our ancestors meant by the expression, I am.'

∞

'There is no more mystery.'

∞

'There is no more misery about our thinking.'

∞

'In wanting to see what we are, it is essential to ask and find out what we are not.'

∞

'We think we are our memories, but these are just thoughts, so if we believe this, we can easily take ourselves to be what we are not. We may think we are what we imagine in the future but this is just thought and is not what we are now.'

∞

'In asking what you are and what you are not, you see you are not your thoughts but consciousness, which is responsible for thoughts.'

∞

'When something is made up it has no authenticity; just as you always know when an actor is acting.'

∞

'The same mistaken authenticity is obvious when our ignorance of believing we are the ego is uncovered.'

∞

'You can see what you are is consciousness of stillness inside you.'

∞

'Consciousness of inner stillness lets us see our inner self is stillness.'

∞

'Consciousness of inner stillness lets us see that our inner self is our natural happiness.'

∞

'Our answer to what we are is I am just 'I am,' the consciousness we all have of inner stillness.'

The sun was setting and they got up to go inside the dwelling. When the sun had set the young woman began to make the second batch of bread.

Whilst kneading the bread she went outside to

see what the day was like. She felt the warm air on her face and arms because of the heat still rising from the hot earth. She knew the cooler night air would slowly appear after two hours and after that, three people would arrive to collect loaves of bread for the next day.

When they had gone, the woman sat with her as they ate the bread she had made along with the vegetables and milk she had exchanged for loaves of bread. As the fire died down they fell asleep in their beds.

◎

The young woman woke and saw the poor light of the pre-dawn darkness. She turned and acknowledged the light again then she slipped out of bed.

She bathed then dressed and went to revive the embers of the fire from the previous night's cooking. She added small dry twigs, then small branches then laid three logs on the smoking logs.

After a breakfast of bread and milk the young woman tidied and cleaned the two small rooms. She then began to make bread. Whilst kneading the bread she went outside to see what the day was like. She felt the cool air on her face and arms because clouds were still hiding the heat and light from the sun. She knew the heat of the day would slowly appear after two hours and after that, three people would arrive to collect loaves of bread for their day.

After the three people had collected their loaves the young woman went around to the back of the house where the woman was sitting the day before.

The woman was sitting still with her eyes closed as the young woman came and sat opposite her.

She saw once again that the woman's face looked more serene than when she had first met her. The young

81

woman had a sense that the calmness and peace in the woman's face was very pure. Again, she could only liken her serene state to the innocence of a flower or the face of a child.

Sitting down opposite her and looking at her, she noticed her thoughts slowed down so much that there was only the occasional thought. She was sitting being still with this woman and not thinking as much as usual.

Several times she would suddenly be aware that she had been in state she could not describe but which was very pleasant. It was neither sleep nor being in a trance, but it was so relaxed she wanted more of it. She felt she didn't want the woman to open her eyes. She felt she didn't want her to leave and go on her journey more south. She too closed her eyes.

Some time after she opened her eyes, she saw the woman also open her eyes and was not at all surprised to see the young woman sitting opposite her.

'How do you meditate?'

'There is not one way to meditate. But there is only one final pathway.'

∞

'There are no techniques to meditate. But there are different levels of attainment in meditation.'

∞

'What we desire to be happy is to stop thoughts, to let us experience our stillness.'

∞

'To meditate we need to withdraw inside to experience this one thing only.'

∞

'There are different levels of attainment in meditation we may be able to experience. Our level of attainment may be different at different times for each of us.'

∞

'If we find it difficult to start by withdrawing inside to see what we are and what we are not, we can turn inwards and gain some control of our mind, our thinking, by tethering it to one thing by following our breathing. It is controlling our mind.'

∞

'Next, we can turn inwards, tethering our mind by repeating a silent sound, a mantra.'

∞

'Meditation shows us we seem conditioned to keep on having thoughts instead of just being still without thoughts.'

∞

'Meditation is mind control, repeatedly stopping thoughts to let us be this inner stillness. The battle resumes every time we meditate. It requires effort. It requires one-pointedness. You need to keep the main aim the main aim.'

∞

'The more we meditate, the more we see thoughts are not us and so the battle of our consciousness against them becomes more effective.'

∞

'To be conscious of what we are as stillness is all we need to do. This consciousness of 'I am' is all we can be.'

∞

'We do not add anything to us to meditate. It is removal. We remove what is not us . . . thought. The reward is the indescribable conscious happiness of stillness.'

∞

'Each time you sit to meditate, ask yourself 'Why am I here?' The answer is 'Only to be happy.' Then ask yourself 'Who you are?' You will see that you are consciousness, not thought. The answers are found inside by being still.'

∞

'The method, path and goal of meditation are contained in the simple statement,' "Be still and know that I am That."

'In other words, searching and seeing inner stillness with no thought is the method. Being conscious of 'I Am' is the only truth. It is all you can be. When you are this you are fully conscious and blissfully happy.'

The sun was setting and they got up to go inside the dwelling. When the sun had set the young woman began to make the second batch of bread.

Whilst kneading the bread she went outside to see what the day was like. She felt the warm air on her face and arms because of the heat still rising from the hot earth. She knew the cooler night air would slowly appear after two hours and after that, three people would arrive to collect loaves of bread for the next day.

When they had gone, the woman sat with her as they ate the bread she had made along with the vegetables and milk she had exchanged for loaves of bread. As the fire died down they fell asleep in their beds.

◎

The young woman woke and saw the poor light of the pre-dawn darkness. She turned and acknowledged the light again then she slipped out of bed.

She bathed then dressed and went to revive the embers of the fire from the previous night's cooking. She added small dry twigs, then small branches then laid three logs on the smoking logs.

After a breakfast of bread and milk the young woman tidied and cleaned the two small rooms. She then began to make bread. Whilst kneading the bread she went outside to see what the day was like. She felt the cool air on her face and arms because clouds were still hiding the heat and light from the sun. She knew the heat of the day would slowly appear after two hours and after that, three people would arrive to collect loaves of bread for their day.

After the three people had collected their loaves the young woman went around to the back of the house where the woman was sitting the day before.

The woman was sitting still with her eyes closed as the young woman came and sat opposite her.

She saw once again that the woman's face looked more serene than when she had first met her. The young woman had a sense that the calmness and peace in the woman's face was very pure. Again, she could only liken her serene state to the innocence of a flower or the face of a child.

Sitting down opposite her and looking at her, she noticed her thoughts slowed down so much that there was only the occasional thought. She was sitting being still with this woman and not thinking as much as usual.

Several times she would suddenly be aware that she had been in state she could not describe but which was very pleasant. It was neither sleep nor being in a trance, but it was so relaxed she wanted more of it. She felt she didn't want the woman to open her eyes. She felt she didn't want her to leave and go on her journey more south. She too closed her eyes.

Some time after she opened her eyes, she saw the woman also open her eyes and was not at all surprised to see the young woman sitting opposite her. After some time the woman spoke.

'You have found your happiness. The old you has been burnt to nothing by the fire of happiness. There are no words for the bliss of stillness.'

The sun was setting and they got up to go inside the dwelling. When the sun had set the young woman began to make the second batch of bread.

Whilst kneading the bread she went outside to see what the day was like. She felt the warm air on her face and arms because of the heat still rising from the hot earth. She knew the cooler night air would slowly appear after two hours and after that, three people would arrive to collect loaves of bread for the next day.

When they had gone, the woman sat with her as they ate the bread she had made along with the vegetables and milk she had exchanged for loaves of bread. As the fire died down they fell asleep in their beds.

◎

The young woman woke and saw the poor light of the pre-dawn darkness. She turned and acknowledged the light again then she slipped out of bed.

She bathed then dressed and went to revive the embers of the fire from the previous night's cooking. She added small dry twigs, then small branches then laid three logs on the smoking logs.

After a breakfast of bread and milk the young woman tidied and cleaned the two small rooms. She then began to make bread. Whilst kneading the bread she went outside to see what the day was like. She felt the cool air on her face and arms because clouds were still hiding the heat and light from the sun. She knew the heat of the day would slowly appear after two hours and after that, three people would arrive to collect loaves of bread for their day.

After the three people had collected their loaves the young woman went around to the back of the house where the woman was sitting the day before.

The woman was sitting still with her eyes closed as the young woman came and sat opposite her.

She saw once again that the woman's face looked more serene than when she had first met her. The young woman had a sense that the calmness and peace in the woman's face was very pure. Again she could only liken her serene state to the innocence of a flower or the face of a child.

Sitting down opposite her and looking at her, she noticed her thoughts slowed down so much that there was only the occasional thought. She was sitting being still with this woman and not thinking as much as usual.

Several times she would suddenly be aware that she had almost been in state she could not describe but which was very pleasant. It was neither sleep nor being in a trance, but it was so relaxed she wanted more of it. She felt she didn't want the woman to open her eyes. She felt she didn't want her to leave and go on her journey more south. She too closed her eyes.

Some time after she opened her eyes, she saw the woman also open her eyes and was not at all surprised to see the young woman sitting opposite her.

'Does solitude help to be happy?'

'Yes. Solitude is an attitude. Solitude lets us detach from the distractions of the world.'

∞

'Solitude lets us detach from the distractions of the world, to experience happiness inside.'

∞

'Seeing our happiness is inside, we begin to spend

more time in solitude and also with those whose view of the world is like ours.'

∞

'Detachment is separating our processes from other people's processes whilst still having a relationship.'

The sun was setting and they got up to go inside the dwelling. When the sun had set the young woman began to make the second batch of bread.

Whilst kneading the bread she went outside to see what the day was like. She felt the warm air on her face and arms because of the heat still rising from the hot earth. She knew the cooler night air would slowly appear after two hours and after that, three people would arrive to collect loaves of bread for the next day.

When they had gone, the woman sat with her as they ate the bread she had made along with the vegetables and milk she had exchanged for loaves of bread. As the fire died down they fell asleep in their beds.

◎

The young woman woke and saw the poor light of the pre-dawn darkness. She turned and acknowledged the light again then she slipped out of bed.

She bathed then dressed and went to revive the embers of the fire from the previous night's cooking. She added small dry twigs, then small branches then laid three logs on the smoking logs.

After a breakfast of bread and milk the young woman tidied and cleaned the two small rooms. She then began to make bread. Whilst kneading the bread she went outside to see what the day was like. She felt the cool air on her face and arms because clouds were still hiding the heat and light from the sun. She knew the heat of the day would slowly appear after two hours and after that, three people would arrive to collect loaves of bread for their day.

After the three people had collected their loaves the young woman went around to the back of the house where the woman was sitting the day before. The woman was sitting still with her eyes closed as the young woman came and sat opposite her.

She saw once again that the woman's face looked more serene than when she had first met her. The young woman had a sense that the calmness and peace in the woman's face was very pure. Again, she could only liken her serene state to the innocence of a flower or the face of a child.

Sitting down opposite her and looking at her, she noticed her thoughts slowed down so much that there was only the occasional thought. She was sitting being still with this woman and not thinking as much as usual.

Several times she would suddenly be aware that she had almost been in state she could not describe but which was very pleasant. It was neither sleep nor being in a trance, but it was so relaxed she wanted more of it.

She felt she didn't want the woman to open her eyes. She felt she didn't want her to leave and go on her journey more south. She too closed her eyes.

Some time after she opened her eyes, she saw the woman also open her eyes and was not at all surprised to see the young woman sitting opposite her.

'What is the most important things about practice?'

'Try and be more and more conscious of 'I am' so that it is your default consciousness. Be one pointed in concentrating on this.'

∞

'Keep the Main Aim the Main Aim.'

∞

The sun was setting and they got up to go inside the dwelling. When the sun had set the young woman began to make the second batch of bread.

Whilst kneading the bread she went outside to see what the day was like. She felt the warm air on her face and arms because of the heat still rising from the hot earth. She knew the cooler night air would slowly appear after two hours and after that, three people would arrive to collect loaves of bread for the next day.

When they had gone, the woman sat with her as they ate the bread she had made along with the vegetables and milk she had exchanged for loaves of bread. As the fire died down they fell asleep in their beds.

◎

The young woman woke and saw the poor light of the pre-dawn darkness. She turned and acknowledged the light again then she slipped out of bed.

She bathed then dressed and went to revive the embers of the fire from the previous night's cooking. She added small dry twigs, then small branches then laid three logs on the smoking logs.

After a breakfast of bread and milk the young woman tidied and cleaned the two small rooms. She then began to make bread. Whilst kneading the bread she went outside to see what the day was like. She felt the cool air on her face and arms because clouds were still hiding the heat and light from the sun. She knew the heat of the day would slowly appear after two hours and after that, three people would arrive to collect loaves of bread for their day.

After the three people had collected their loaves the young woman went around to the back of the house where the woman was sitting the day before.

The woman was sitting still with her eyes closed as the young woman came and sat opposite her.

She saw once again that the woman's face looked more serene than when she had first met her. The young woman had a sense that the calmness and peace in the woman's face was very pure. Again, she could only liken her serene state to the innocence of a flower or the face of a child.

Sitting down opposite her and looking at her she noticed her thoughts slowed down so much that there was only the occasional thought. She was sitting being still with this woman and not thinking as much as usual.

Several times she would suddenly be aware that she had been in state she could not describe but which was very pleasant. It was neither sleep nor being in a trance, but it was so relaxed she wanted more of it. She felt she didn't want the woman to open her eyes. She felt she didn't want her to leave and go on her journey more south. She too closed her eyes.

Some time after she opened her eyes, she saw the woman also open her eyes and was not at all surprised to see the young woman sitting opposite her. After some time the woman spoke.

'There are no words for stillness.'

The sun was setting and they got up to go inside the dwelling. When the sun had set the young woman began to make the second batch of bread.

Whilst kneading the bread she went outside to see what the day was like. She felt the warm air on her face and arms because of the heat still rising from the hot earth. She knew the cooler night air would slowly appear after two hours and after that, three people would arrive to collect loaves of bread for the next day.

When they had gone, the woman sat with her as they ate the bread she had made along with the vegetables and milk she had exchanged for loaves of bread. As the fire died down they fell asleep in their beds.

◎

The young woman woke and saw the poor light of the pre-dawn darkness. She turned and acknowledged the light again then she slipped out of bed.

She bathed then dressed and went to revive the embers of the fire from the previous night's cooking. She added small dry twigs, then small branches then laid three logs on the smoking logs.

After a breakfast of bread and milk the young woman tidied and cleaned the two small rooms. She then began to make bread. Whilst kneading the bread she went outside to see what the day was like. She felt the cool air on her face and arms because clouds were still hiding the heat and light from the sun. She knew the heat of the day would slowly appear after two hours and after that, three people would arrive to collect loaves of bread for their day.

After the three people had collected their loaves the young woman went around to the back of the house where the woman was sitting the day before.

The woman was sitting still with her eyes closed as the young woman came and sat opposite her.

She saw once again that the woman's face looked more serene than when she had first met her. The young woman had a sense that the calmness and peace in the woman's face was very pure. Again, she could only liken her serene state to the innocence of a flower or the face of a child.

Sitting down opposite her and looking at her, she noticed her thoughts slowed down so much that there was only the occasional thought. She was sitting being still with this woman and not thinking as much as usual.

Several times she would suddenly be aware that she had been in state she could not describe but which was very pleasant. It was neither sleep nor being in a trance, but it was so relaxed she wanted more of it. She felt she didn't want the woman to open her eyes. She felt she didn't want her to leave and go on her journey more south. She too closed her eyes.

Some time after she opened her eyes, she saw the woman also open her eyes and was not at all surprised to see the young woman sitting opposite her. Even after some time the woman did not speak.

The sun was setting and they got up to go inside the dwelling. When the sun had set the young woman began to make the second batch of bread.

Whilst kneading the bread she went outside to see what the day was like. She felt the warm air on her face and arms because of the heat still rising from the hot earth. She knew the cooler night air would slowly appear after two hours and after that, three people would arrive to collect loaves of bread for the next day.

When they had gone the woman sat with her as they ate the bread she had made along with the vegetables and milk she had exchanged for loaves of bread. As the fire

94

died down they fell asleep in their beds.

◎

The young woman woke and saw the poor light of the pre-dawn darkness. She turned and acknowledged the light again then she slipped out of bed.

She bathed then dressed and went to revive the embers of the fire from the previous night's cooking. She added small dry twigs, then small branches then laid three logs on the smoking logs.

After a breakfast of bread and milk the young woman tidied and cleaned the two small rooms. She then began to make bread. Whilst kneading the bread she went outside to see what the day was like. She felt the cool air on her face and arms because clouds were still hiding the heat and light from the sun. She knew the heat of the day would slowly appear after two hours and after that, three people would arrive to collect loaves of bread for their day.

After the three people had collected their loaves the young woman went around to the back of the house where the woman was sitting the day before.

The woman was sitting still with her eyes closed as the young woman came and sat opposite her.

She saw once again that the woman's face looked more serene than when she had first met her. The young woman had a sense that the calmness and peace in the woman's face was very pure. Again, she could only liken her serene state to the innocence of a flower or the face of a child.

Sitting down opposite her and looking at her, she noticed her thoughts slowed down so much that there was only the occasional thought. She was sitting being still with this woman and not thinking as much as usual.

Several times she would suddenly be aware that she had been in state she could not describe but which was very pleasant. It was neither sleep nor being in a trance, but it was so relaxed she wanted more of it. She felt she didn't want the woman to open her eyes. She felt she didn't want her to leave and go on her journey more south. She too closed her eyes.

Some time after she opened her eyes, she saw the woman was not there. She continued to sit in stillness with her eyes closed.

The sun was setting and she got up to go inside the dwelling. When the sun had set the young woman began to make the second batch of bread.

Whilst kneading the bread she went outside to see what the day was like. She felt the warm air on her face and arms because of the heat still rising from the hot earth. She knew the cooler night air would slowly appear after two hours and after that, three people would arrive to collect loaves of bread for the next day.

When they had gone, the young woman sat and ate the bread she had made along with the vegetables and milk she had exchanged for loaves of bread. As the fire died down she fell asleep in her bed.

◎

The young woman woke and saw the poor light of the pre-dawn darkness. She turned and acknowledged the light again then she slipped out of bed.

She bathed then dressed and went to revive the embers of the fire from the previous night's cooking. She added small dry twigs, then small branches then laid three logs on the smoking logs.

After a breakfast of bread and milk the young woman tidied and cleaned the two small rooms. She then began to make bread. Whilst kneading the bread she went outside to see what the day was like. She felt the cool air on her face and arms because clouds were still hiding the heat and light from the sun. She knew the heat of the day would slowly appear after two hours and after that, three people would arrive to collect loaves of bread for their day.

After the three people had collected their loaves the young woman went around to the back of the house where the woman had sat the day before.

Sitting down she noticed her thoughts slowed down so much that she was aware there were no more thoughts. She was sitting being still. She was conscious of her happiness but she could not see that it radiated from her eyes like a beacon.

Some time after she opened her eyes. She saw a young woman. The young woman had brought her bread. She continued to sit in stillness with her eyes closed.

◎

The woman woke and saw the poor light of the pre-dawn darkness. She turned and acknowledged the light again then she slipped out of bed.

She bathed then dressed and went outside to the back of the dwelling and sat on a log in the cool morning.

She felt the presence of the woman who had sat there with her for many days. Her presence was stronger, as if they were the same consciousness.

Sitting down she noticed her thoughts had slowed down so much that she was aware there were no more thoughts. She was sitting being still.

Later when she opened her eyes she saw some young

97

women were sitting around her. She saw their yearning for the happiness she had discovered inside.

They had brought her bread, milk and vegetables. She closed her eyes and continued to sit in stillness.

∞

3.

The Teacher

Like Groundhog Day, it can seem that repeated effort keeps on returning us to the same place. But with perseverance, eventually we see who we are.

The boy was tired but kept on walking until mid- morning. He realised that he was tired because he had been walking so much, so he stopped for some refreshment and to rest.

He found a place to drink some water. It had a bench behind a table facing the road, which was steaming from the hot sun.

Some time after he sat down, he noticed a man on the other end of the long wooden bench. He was wearing baggy khaki trousers and a khaki shirt.

The man smiled and nodded at the boy sitting on the other end of the bench.

As he smiled, a single tear ran from the corner of each eye down each cheek, which he quickly wiped.

The boy noticed how happy this stranger seemed, even though he was old and on his own. He wondered for a while how anyone could be so happy.

When the man smiled at the boy and nodded, the boy noticed him wiping a tear from either eye. The boy could see these were tears of happiness.

There was no conversation as neither talked. The boy's head was full of concerns about his future. His eyes looked this way and then the other way. He was a little fidgety and not particularly calm. He was not concerned with the old man.

As he thought about the next part of his walking, he realised how tired he was. He was worried he would never find a home and this made him worry that he would never be happy.

The old man was calm and sat quite still as he looked out from the table onto the road outside. His mind was free of thoughts as he stared straight ahead. He was not concerned about the future. He was not concerned about anything. He was minding his own business and detached from everything in the outside world. He was as happy as he could be as he sat smiling, looking straight ahead onto the road outside.

Again the boy noticed how happy this stranger seemed, even though he was old and on his own. He wondered for a while how anyone could be so happy.

After some time, the man felt rested and straightened his skinny legs, rose from the bench and left. The boy sat looking ahead at the road for some time. He finished his cool drink and realised it was mid-morning. He thought he should get walking on the hot dusty road again to make progress.

◎

After two hours of walking, the heat from the bright hot midday sun forced the boy to find more water. He saw a similar sheltered building in the distance and quickened his pace in anticipation of quenching his thirst.

Like the previous building, it was dark but he found a long wooden bench behind a table facing the road and sat down. As his eyes adjusted from the bright sunlight to the unlit coolness of the building, he saw that the man from his previous stop had got there before him and was sitting on the end of his bench.

There was no conversation as neither talked. The boy's head was still full of concerns about his future. His eyes looked this way and then the other way. He was a little fidgety and not particularly calm. He was not concerned with the old man.

As he thought about the next part of his walking, he realised how tired he was. He was worried he would never find a home and this made him worry that he would never be happy.

The old man was calm and sat quite still as he looked

out from the table onto the road outside. His mind was free of thoughts as he stared straight ahead. He was not concerned about the future. He was not concerned about anything. He was minding his own business and detached from everything in the outside world. He was as happy as he could be as he sat smiling, looking straight ahead onto the road outside.

The boy noticed again how happy this stranger seemed, even though he was old and on his own. He wondered for a while how anyone could be so happy and once again he realised he didn't have any answers to how he could be as happy.

After some time, the man felt rested and straightened his skinny legs, rose from the bench and left. The boy sat looking ahead at the road for some time. He finished his cool drink and realised it was past midday. He thought he should begin walking on the hot dusty road again to make progress.

◎

After two hours of walking, the heat from the bright hot early afternoon sun forced the boy to find more water. He saw a similar sheltered building in the distance and quickened his pace in anticipation of quenching his thirst.

Like the previous building, it was dark but he found a long wooden bench behind a table facing the road and sat down. As his eyes adjusted from the bright sunlight to the unlit coolness of the building, once again he saw that the man from his previous stop had got there before him and was sitting on the end of his bench.

There was no conversation as neither talked. The boy's head was full of concerns about his future. His eyes looked this way and then the other way. He was a little fidgety and not particularly calm. He was not concerned with the old man. Instead, his mind turned to how tired he was. He was worried he would never find a home and this made him worry that he would never be happy.

The old man was calm and sat quite still as he looked out from the table onto the road outside. His mind was free of thoughts as he stared straight ahead. He was not concerned about the future. He was not concerned about anything. He was minding his own business and detached from everything in the outside world. He was as happy as he could be as he sat smiling, looking straight ahead onto the road outside.

The boy noticed again how happy this stranger seemed, even though he was old and on his own. He wondered for a while how anyone could be so happy and once again he realised he didn't have any answers to how he could be as happy.

But he was also curious and even though he was a little reluctant to strike up conversations with strangers, he asked the man.

'How come you seem so happy?'

'I am happy because I work hard just to be happy.' He looked at the boy then looked straight ahead. After some time, the man felt rested and straightened his skinny legs, rose from the bench and left.

The boy sat at the table for some time, looking ahead at the road. He finished his cool drink and realised it was past the middle of the afternoon. He thought he should begin walking on the hot dusty road again to make progress.

When he stood outside in the sun, he saw the man walking ahead of him, but he forgot about him. He started wondering if he would ever be that happy. He wanted that more than anything else he could think of.

After two hours of walking, the heat from his walking in the late afternoon sun forced him to find more water. He saw a similar sheltered building in the distance and quickened his pace in anticipation of quenching his thirst.

Like the previous building, it was dark but he found a long wooden bench behind a table facing the road and sat down. As his eyes adjusted from the bright sunlight to the unlit coolness of the building, once again he saw that the man from his previous stop had got there before him and was sitting on the end of his bench.

There was no conversation as neither talked. The boy's head was full of concerns about his future. His eyes looked this way and then the other way. He was a little fidgety and not particularly calm. He was not concerned with the old man.

As he thought about the next part of his walking, he realised how tired he was. He was worried he would never find a home and this made him worry that he would never be happy.

The old man was calm and sat quite still as he looked out from the table onto the road outside. His mind was free of thoughts as he stared straight ahead. He was not concerned about the future. He was not concerned about anything. He was minding his own business and detached from everything in the outside world. He was as happy as he could be as he sat smiling, looking straight ahead onto the road outside.

The boy noticed again how happy this stranger seemed, even though he was old and on his own. He wondered for a while how anyone could be so happy and once again he realised he didn't have any answers to how he could be as happy.

'I saw you walking in front me. How did you get here so much before me?'

'I saw you walking behind me. I knew you were already following my path. I don't mean the actual physical path you take when you are walking, even though it seems that way. You are about to follow the path in life I took.'

'How do you know that?'

'I have been where you are now going. I did it in the past and you will do it in the future. But we are both here now. Whichever way you go, you will be following me. So, I will be there with you.'

After some time, the man felt rested and straightened his skinny legs, rose from the bench and left.

The boy sat at the table looking ahead at the road for some time. He finished his cool drink and realised it was late afternoon. He thought he should begin walking on the hot dusty road again to make progress.

When he stood outside in the sun, he saw the man walking ahead of him, but he forgot about him. He started wondering if he would ever be that happy. He wanted that more than anything else he could think of. He was determined to ask the man more about this if he met him again.

◎

After two hours of walking, the heat from the bright hot early morning sun forced the boy to find more water. He saw a similar sheltered building in the distance and quickened his pace in anticipation of quenching his thirst.

Like the previous building, it was dark but he found a long wooden bench behind a table facing the road and sat down. As his eyes adjusted from the bright sunlight to the unlit coolness of the building, once again he saw that the man from his previous stop had got there before him and was sitting on the end of his bench.

There was no conversation as neither talked. The boy's head was full of concerns about his future. His eyes looked this way and then the other way. He was a little fidgety and not particularly calm. He was not concerned with the old man.

As he thought about the next part of his walking, he realised how tired he was. He was worried he would never find a home and this made him worry that he would never be happy.

The old man was calm and sat quite still as he looked out from the table onto the road outside. His mind was free of thoughts as he stared straight ahead. He was not concerned about the future. He was not concerned about anything. He was minding his own business and detached from everything in the outside world. He was as happy as he could be as he sat smiling, looking straight ahead onto the road outside.

The boy noticed again how happy this stranger seemed, even though he was old and on his own. He wondered for a while how anyone could be so happy and once again he realised he didn't have any answers to how he could be as happy.

'I know I asked you this before but how do you work hard just to be happy?'

'After finding that you can't find happiness outside.'

'I don't understand.'

'When you realise that the only real happiness is inside yourself, you have to work hard to uncover it.'

'Does it take long?

'Time does not come into it. It always takes effort.' He was smiling gently.

After some time the man felt rested and straightened his skinny legs, rose from the bench and left.

The boy sat at the table looking ahead at the road for some time. He finished his cool drink and realised it was past the middle of the morning. He thought he should begin walking on the hot dusty road again to make progress.

When he stood outside in the sun, he saw the man walking ahead of him, but he forgot about him. He started wondering if he would ever be that happy. He wanted that more than anything else he could think of. He was determined to ask the man more about this if he met him again.

◎

After two hours of late morning walking, the heat from the midday sun forced him to find refreshments. He saw a sheltered building in the distance and quickened his pace in anticipation of quenching his thirst.

Like the previous buildings, it was dark but he found a long wooden bench behind a table facing the road and sat down. As his eyes adjusted from the bright sunlight to the unlit coolness of the building he could see he was on his own.

As he thought about the next part of his walking, he realised how tired he was. He was worried he would never find a home and this made him worry that he would never be happy.

Just after he started his cold drink, the old man came and sat on the other end of the long wooden bench he was sitting on.

There was no conversation as neither talked. The old man was calm and sat quite still as he looked out from the table onto the road outside. His mind was free of thoughts as he stared straight ahead. He was not concerned about the future. He was not concerned about anything. He was minding his own business and quite detached from others. He was as happy as he could be as he sat smiling, looking straight ahead onto the road outside.

The more the boy thought about how calm and happy the old man seemed, the less he wanted to pursue his questioning from the day before. Just sitting with him made him feel a little easier about himself so, he sat and felt even better about himself.

The longer he sat, the more he realised that the man sitting with him was somehow showing him how to be happy.

Eventually the old man raised himself to his feet, looked at the boy, smiled and left.

The boy sat at the table looking ahead at the road for some time. He finished his cool drink and realised it was much later than he thought. Most of the day had passed and it was now late afternoon. He thought he should begin the last walk of the day.

◎

The old man was calm and sat quite still as he looked out from the table onto the road outside. His mind was free of thoughts as he stared straight ahead. He was not concerned about the future. He was not concerned about anything. He was minding his own business and de-tached from everything in the outside world. He was as happy as he could be as he sat smiling, looking straight ahead onto the road outside.

Once more, as the boy thought about the how calm and happy the old man seemed, the less he wanted to pursue questioning him. He realised that he felt strangely calm when he was in this man's presence. But because of this new feeling of inner calmness and especially because only yesterday he had sat with the old man for hours without talking, he felt he should mention this.

'Yesterday I felt the calmest I have ever felt. My childhood was chaotic and so there was never inner security or the feeling of calmness like I felt yesterday. I felt that the damage, the hole inside me from my childhood had somehow been filled in. What is this calmness?'

'It does not have a good enough name because words can't describe it adequately enough.' The old man was staring straight ahead into the distance. 'It is being conscious of your own inner stillness. What you were conscious of is your very nature. Your nature is not to have thoughts and to be still.'

The boy considered what the man said for some time and felt he had to ask him more whilst he was still with him.

'I was so surprised that inside there is a part of me that is so happy. How can I be in that state longer, I mean every day? How do I get to know that part of me better?'

There was silence as the man looked straight ahead. Eventually he turned to the boy, looked at him, smiled and spoke.

'If you are hungry enough for it, you will make the effort to have it. It requires effort at wanting just stillness. Some have suffered so much that healing the damage from their childhood is the most important aim of their life. As you said, it helps to heal your suffering, to fill in the hole inside you from your childhood, the hole in your soul.'

'I know deep inside me what you say is right. But how do I find out more?'

'If you pursue this, you will uncover it.' The old

man raised himself to his feet and left. The boy sat at the table looking ahead at the road for some time. He finished his cool drink and realised he should carry on with the rest of the morning walk.

◎

After two hours of walking, tiredness forced the boy to find refreshments. He saw a sheltered building in the distance and quickened his pace in anticipation of quenching his thirst. But inside there was nowhere to sit. There was someone in every possible seat.

'Why are you all here?' He asked an elderly man.
'We are having a meeting with a local leader.'
'Is it soon?'
'Yes, it will start in a short while.'
'Will it last long?'
'Sometimes all evening, late into the night.'

The boy waited with them for some time but he saw that he was not going to have peace and rest in a group of people, so he left and walked back onto the road.

After a short while he saw another refreshment building and was relieved to find it was empty. He found a long wooden bench behind a table facing the road and sat down.

He felt at peace away from the gossip which was all about what had been and about what might be. Away from the turmoil of competitive thinking amongst this group, he was now closer to his own self. He was calmer.

He looked out on to the road. He considered what he should be doing. He thought about what the old man had said and wondered what he should do to find happiness. The words the man had said echoed in his head, 'When you realise that the only real happiness is inside yourself, you have to work hard to uncover it. Time does not come into it.' Then he had said, 'It always takes effort. If you pursue this, you will uncover it.'

'What is the work?' the boy thought. 'How do I look inside myself? It's not like I can read about me like reading a book. He never said how to do it.'

He felt lost. He trusted this man as neither had any investment in the other. They had nothing material to gain form the other. He trusted him because when he asked him about his happiness, he did not try and sell it to him.

As he was thinking this, he saw from the dark area behind him a man moving towards the other end of the wooden bench. It was the old man in the khaki trousers and shirt.

The old man was calm and sat quite still as he looked out from the table onto the road outside. His mind seemed free of thoughts as he stared straight ahead. He didn't seem concerned about anything. He was minding his own business and quite detached from others. He didn't seem worried about anything. He appeared to be as happy as he could be as he sat smiling, looking straight ahead onto the road outside.

'I need your help. You said if I tried to uncover my happiness, I would find it. Since we spoke, I have thought about nothing else other than this. But I don't feel I am getting any closer to being happy.' The boy noticed the old man had a gentle smile on his face as he continued to stare straight ahead for some time.

'You have seen that your happiness is inside you already. Happiness is your nature. This is one of the most important achievements anyone can make in their life. You have thought a lot about happiness but your happiness can't be uncovered by thinking about it. Thinking is the actual veil which hides it. When you can stop thinking, even for a few seconds, you will see that in the space between your last thought and the next one that comes, there is just consciousness, stillness, without any thought.'

'How do I do that?'

'You can only be it. It is achieved by ceaseless effort to be it. You have to have a hunger for happiness like there is nothing else you desire.'

'How do I make the effort?'

'Your mind needs to be controlled by you so it is not wondering off in a different direction of thought every few moments. Only when it is still, can you see what you are.'

'I don't understand. How do I do this?'

'First, mind control. Then the aim is to find out what you are by being still.'

'How do I control my mind and how can I be still?'

'Try it on your own. This needs repeated and ceaseless daily focusing the mind on this one thing. At the same time, you also have to live and eat. But giving yourself times when you are still every day is the most important thing you can do. It is vital.' His eyes looked straight ahead, then he turned to the boy, smiled and left.

◎

The boy didn't begin his early morning walk as usual. Instead, he sat upright where he had slept and looked at what the old man had said. As he stared ahead, he tried to look at what he was.

'Am I my parent's son? No, I am not just that. Am I this person on a daily path of discovery? No, I am more than that.' He closed his eyes to see clearer inside. 'Ok so I am not just my parent's son, or this person on a path of discovery. I am not those. So what am I?'

After tiring himself with this question he got up to

begin his walking.

As he walked he kept on asking himself the same question, 'What am I?' After some time he became so lost for ways to see himself clearly that he looked for somewhere to rest.

He was feeling disappointed he had not been able to make any progress with looking inside for happiness. He didn't want to think about it anymore, so he gave up and just stared ahead as he walked along the road.

But the question arose more than once which he could not avoid, 'What am I?' At first, there was an answer, 'I am my memories and I am my hopes for a happy future.' Then he realised that he was looking at things outside himself. He tried to look inwards but felt blocked. Next he became distracted by the conditions of where he was walking.

The day was showing signs of rain, so he thought he would look for cover in a building. After a while he came to a rest house, but in it were many people who had also sensed the drop in air pressure along with the darkening skies. It was not full and he could have taken refuge from the oncoming rain but he did not want to spend the afternoon and perhaps the night in a crowded room.

'You should stay here.' Said a middle aged man as he walked past it. 'There isn't another shelter like this for miles, except for ruined ones. There's a whole night of rain coming. It could last for days. You'll get drenched if you carry on.'

The boy put his hand up to thank him and carried on walking.

He quickened his pace at the warning of the man. Most of the refreshment houses were an hour or two hours apart but sometimes there were ones in between which had been abandoned, usually because of dilapidation.

Soon after midday had passed, he felt an occasional drop of rain on his face and head. He could see what looked like an abandoned refreshment house just ahead.

Knowing he was not going to make it there dry, he surrendered. He relaxed and welcomed the rain which he felt was about to become puddles and rivers by his feet. A few moments later, rain was streaming down his face and his shoes were full of rain water. He looked up at the sky which was dark everywhere, apart from an area ahead, far beyond where he was walking. In the midst of this torrential downpour, suddenly he felt as if he was being shown that the path ahead was positive and the right one to have taken. He smiled and walked with his arms out wide, welcoming not just the rain but whatever life was.

◎

Unlike the previous refreshment buildings, it was not so dark because of a hole in the roof and there was no one there. He found a toppled over long wooden bench behind an upturned table which he straightened up. He sat on the bench facing the road. He looked around him and as he turned back to face the road, he saw the old man in khaki enter through the door and sit at the other end of the wooden bench.

The old man was calm and sat quite still as he looked out from the table onto the road outside. His mind was free of thoughts as he stared straight ahead. He was not concerned about the future. He was not concerned about anything. He was minding his own business and detached from everything in the outside world. He was as happy as he could be as he sat smiling, looking straight ahead onto the road outside.

After a long time, the man turned to look at him. They exchanged an almost identical smile as they sat in silence.

The boy broke the long silence.

'How do you not have thoughts?'

'Thoughts are seen and stopped by going inside to look inwards.'

'I tried looking today. At first I was looking outwards at what I am. Then I started looking inwards but I was blocked. I couldn't see a way inside.'

'When you are looking outside, if it is dark, you can't see, so you turn the lights on, then you can see. When you are looking inside, you can't see if it is light with distractions from outside, so you turn the outer lights off by closing your eyes. Only then you begin to see.'

The boy closed his eyes and sat still.

◎

The boy woke from his sleep and immediately sat on the bench and closed his eyes. After some hours sitting on and off with his eyes closed he was aware of the faint sound of the man in khaki sitting down at the other end of the wooden bench.

The boy opened his eyes. After a long time, the man turned to look at him. They exchanged an almost identical smile as they sat in silence.

The old man was calm and sat quite still as he looked out from the table onto the road outside. His mind was free of thoughts as he stared straight ahead. He was not concerned about the future. He was not concerned about anything. He was minding his own business and detached from everything in the outside world. He was as happy as

116

he could be as he sat smiling, looking straight ahead onto the road outside.

The boy broke the long silence.

'At first all I could see were blurred red patterns in front of my eyes. Then my eyeball stopped moving but then I noticed my thoughts were coming one after another. I couldn't stop them easily, even when I tried hard. They just surface from nowhere.'

'Each of us experiences this when we begin. But when the mind is tethered like an animal to one spot, it does not cause problems, so thoughts do not keep on appearing so easily. What is needed is mind control.

'How do I tether my thoughts so they stop appearing?

'The mind can be tethered so thoughts stop appearing so quickly. You either tether it by following your breathing or repeating a sound. A sound is easier so I will let you hear one. When thoughts appear, bring back the sound to the front of your consciousness. However, thoughts will always try and appear.'

He turned to the boy and pronounced a sound. He leant towards the boy, nodding his head he invited him with his upturned right hand to repeat the sound, which the boy did.

The man in khaki said the sound softer and also indicated by lowering his downturned hand nearer and nearer to the floor to say it lower and softer, which the boy did. The man then indicated to say the sound more quietly, which the boy again did.

Once again the man indicated that the boy should say it even quieter, which the boy did. When the boy was saying it silently but still moving his lips, the man indicated with his fingers running down over his eyes that the boy should close his eyes, which the boy did.

Some time later the boy opened his eyes and looked straight ahead into the distance. He didn't move and his breathing was still very slow. Then he closed his eyes again, silently producing the sound inside. Later he opened his eyes and looked straight ahead, then he spoke.

'I have never felt so happy. I feel at peace. I am the calmest I have ever been. After a while thoughts did come but bringing back the sound made them go.' He was radiating a smile which the old man recognised.

'This is meditation. It is this simple. It should be your first mental activity of each day and it should be repeated as often as you can do it throughout the day.' As soon as he said this he looked at the boy, smiled and walked outside as there was a break in the storm.

◎

The boy woke from his sleep and immediately sat on the bench and closed his eyes. After some hours he was aware of the faint sound of the man in khaki sitting down at the other end of the wooden bench. He opened his eyes.

After a long time, the man turned to look at him. They exchanged an almost identical smile as they sat in silence.

The old man was calm and sat quite still as he looked out from the table onto the road outside. His mind was free of thoughts as he stared straight ahead. He was not concerned about the future. He was not concerned about anything. He was minding his own business and detached from everything in the outside world. He was as happy as he could be as he sat smiling, looking straight ahead onto the road outside.

The boy broke the long silence.

'I now see what you explained to me. I feel I have

more control over thoughts coming and going. There's also a deep peace I can't describe. It is just peace.'

'Meditation is an activity to purify the mind so it is controlled. When it is controlled you can then begin to be more conscious of what you are. Now you know how to control your mind with meditation, you can begin to ask what you are.

'How do you find out what you are?'

'You have to know the Self in yourself by yourself. This is the highest state. Your nature is happiness. Your nature is a state of consciousness which is happiness.

Our difficulty seeing this is because it is veiled by our ignorance. We are born happy. But, we see suffering and we experience suffering. We are told that we can be made happy again by the world. But this does not work. We are told we will succeed if we work hard. But this does not work.

We are conditioned and programmed by this ignorance so much that we lose touch with our inner happiness.

We have to work hard to get back in touch with our natural consciousness, our state of inner happiness. We have to remove the darkness, the ignorance that the world wants us to believe. Knowledge leads to the path of release from suffering, ignorance to worldly pursuits of all possessions.'

'I find it difficult to understand how to do this.'

'Asking what you are is the process of removing your ignorance so that you can see your inner state of happiness.

We have to ask what we are, our whole life. That question must be at the forefront of your consciousness so that your happiness is your main priority. It is not that you have to keep on asking yourself the same question all the time, What am I? But that you constantly try and be what you are and avoid what you are not.

Hearing this is vital. Reflecting on this is more powerful. Being this is many times more powerful.'

'When is the best time to do this?'

'Now and all the time. When you sit quietly with your eyes closed and you battle your thoughts so that they go, what is left is your consciousness without thoughts, the Witness.

When at other times you are active with your eyes open, do the same. You find out what you actually are by eliminating what you are not.

As soon as he said this he looked at the boy, smiled and walked outside as there was a break in the storm.

◎

The boy had been walking all morning and saw a rest house ahead of him. He slowed down to look and saw the man in khaki standing outside. The boy walked towards him and as he did so, he noticed the old man was looking at him with the gentle smile he always had when he sat with him. The man beckoned with his hand for the boy to come into the rest house.

Once inside, they sat at either end or a wooden bench behind a table. They both stared ahead at first. Then they both closed their eyes. After some hours the boy straightened himself up and looked at the old man who on hearing the rustling of the boy, also opened his eyes.

The old man was calm and sat quite still as he looked out from the table onto the road outside. His mind was free of thoughts as he stared straight ahead. He was not concerned about the future. He was not concerned about anything. He was minding his own business and detached

from everything in the outside world. He was as happy as he could be as he sat smiling, looking straight ahead onto the road outside.

'I am still not clear about what I am.' The boy said.

'Try looking for the answer by elimination. When you ask what you are, try identifying what you are not. You only find out what you actually are by eliminating what you are not. This is removing your ignorance.

You might consider your body to be you but using anything attached to the five senses to be yourself is like holding onto a crocodile's tale to cross a river. When you see what you are not, only then can you see what you are.'

◎

When the man in Khaki had gone, the boy closed his eyes and followed what the man had suggested. He continued this path which he now knew was his path. He sat in still-ness for hours every day.

After days in the same rest house, the boy decided to move on and walk back on the road. He had not seen the man in khaki since he told him about the crocodile's tail and he wanted his help.

He had spent much of every day looking at what he was and what he was not, both with his eyes closed and with his eyes open.

He now saw that he was at another block in finding out what he was. He felt he was not finding out about his inner self and so he went back on the road to see if he would meet up with the man.

He set off walking in the early morning warmth and by the middle of the afternoon he was sitting in the third rest house of the day.

He sat with his closed eyes using the sound the man

had given him to make thoughts less frequent until there were some moments without them. During these moments he felt a deep peace.

He was brought to open his eyes by the sense that the man was sitting on the end of the wooden bench he was sitting on.

After a long time, the man turned to look at him. They exchanged an almost identical smile as they sat in silence.

The old man was calm and sat quite still as he looked out from the table onto the road outside. His mind was free of thoughts as he stared straight ahead. He was not concerned about the future. He was not concerned about anything. He was minding his own business and detached from everything in the outside world. He was as happy as he could be as he sat smiling, looking straight ahead onto the road outside.

The boy broke the long silence.

'I keep on getting distracted by all sorts of thoughts. A lot of the thoughts are to do with small fears.'

'Fear of losing what we see as being us and ours is overcome by keeping up the questioning of what we are.

Acquiring possessions such as money, things, power, influence or knowledge to make you happy makes you unhappy because all possessions lead to fear of their use and loss. Fear and loss make us think we will be happier if we can more securely possess them, so an endless pursuit begins. Loss anxiety makes us try harder to possess what does not even make us happy. This applies to the very small as well as the big things in our life. All these things keep our thoughts going.'

◎

When the man in Khaki had gone, the boy closed his eyes and followed what the man had suggested. He continued walking his path. He sat in stillness for hours every day.

After many days in the same rest house, the boy decided to move on and walk back on the road. He had not seen the man in khaki since he told him about the thoughts of small fears and now he wanted his help again.

He had spent much of every day looking at what he was and what he was not, both with his eyes closed and with his eyes open.

He now saw that he was at another block in finding out what he was. He felt he was not finding out about his inner self and so he went back on the road to see if he would meet up with the man.

He set off walking in the early morning warmth and by the middle of the afternoon he was sitting in the third rest house of the day.

He sat with closed eyes using the sound the man had given him to make thoughts less frequent until there were some moments without them. During these brief moments he felt a deep peace.

He was brought to open his eyes by the sense that the man was sitting on the end of the wooden bench, which he was.

After a long time, the man turned to look at him. They exchanged an almost identical smile as they sat in silence.

The old man was calm and sat quite still as he looked out from the table onto the road outside. His mind was free of thoughts as he stared straight ahead. He was not concerned about the future. He was not concerned about anything. He was minding his own business and detached from everything in the outside world. He was as happy as he could be as he sat smiling, looking straight ahead onto the road outside.

The boy broke the long silence.

'I am stuck again. I keep getting thoughts about the most peaceful state I can be in. I also get thoughts of the most beautiful place I could be.'

'Don't be misled by beauty because Beauty is something recognised outside, happiness is always inside. Happiness is what you desire most.

Don't be misled by beauty because beauty is derived from the senses, happiness is revealed inside.

Don't be misled by beauty because beauty is a synthesis of fine thinking, happiness is simply being in the heart with no thoughts.

Happiness is your only desire. To uncover this you need to give up all else. You have learnt how to have much more control of your mind.

When you have moments of stillness when there are no thoughts, ask what you are. You will see you are not your thoughts. You will see you are not a bundle of thoughts. You will see you are the witness of thoughts. Being conscious of being the witness is just being.'

◎

When the man in Khaki had gone, the boy closed his eyes and followed what the man had suggested. He continued walking his path. He sat in stillness for hours every day.

After many days in the same rest house, the boy decided to move on and walk back on the road. He had not seen the man in khaki since he told him about being the witness and now he wanted his help again.

He had spent much of every day looking at what he was and what he was not, both with his eyes closed and with his eyes open.

He now saw that he was at another block in finding out what he was. He felt he was not finding out about his inner self and so he went back on the road to see if he would meet up with the man.

He set off walking in the early morning warmth and by the middle of the afternoon he was sitting in the third rest house of the day.

He sat with closed eyes using the sound the man had given him to make thoughts less frequent until there were some moments without them. During these brief moments he felt a deep peace.

He was brought to open his eyes by the sense that the man was sitting on the end of the wooden bench, which he was.

After a long time, the man turned to look at him. They exchanged an almost identical smile as they sat in silence.

The old man was calm and sat quite still as he looked out from the table onto the road outside. His mind was free of thoughts as he stared straight ahead. He was not concerned about the future. He was not concerned about anything. He was minding his own business and detached from everything in the outside world. He was as happy as he could be as he sat smiling, looking straight ahead onto the road outside.

The boy broke the long silence.

'I am stuck again. I keep on getting thoughts. But they are not really about anything, just memories of the past and worry about the future.'

'You might see you as being your past memories or your future dreams. These are just thoughts and not you.

The past and future are not you. The past and future do not exist. Only your consciousness exists about you. Your consciousness can only exist in the present. Staying

125

in the present gets rid of the past and future.

Keep on with this until you eliminate everything that you are not. Including your thoughts.'

◎

When the man in Khaki had gone, the boy closed his eyes and followed what the man had suggested. He continued walking his path. He sat in stillness for hours every day.

After many days in the same rest house, the boy decided to move on and walk back on the road. He had not seen the man in khaki since he told him about staying in the present and now he wanted his help again.

He had spent much of every day looking at what he was and what he was not, both with his eyes closed and with his eyes open.

He now saw that he was at another block in finding out what he was. He felt he was not finding out about his inner self and so he went back on the road to see if he would meet up with the man.

He set off walking in the early morning warmth and by the middle of the afternoon he was sitting in the third rest house of the day.

He sat with closed eyes using the sound the man had given him to make thoughts less frequent until there were some moments without them. During these brief moments he felt a deep peace.

He was brought to open his eyes by the sense that the man was sitting on the end of the wooden bench, which he was.

After a long time, the man turned to look at him. They exchanged an almost identical smile as they sat in silence.

The old man was calm and sat quite still as he looked

126

out from the table onto the road outside. His mind was free of thoughts as he stared straight ahead. He was not concerned about the future. He was not concerned about anything. He was minding his own business and detached from everything in the outside world. He was as happy as he could be as he sat smiling, looking straight ahead onto the road outside.

The boy broke the long silence.

'I am stuck again. I keep on getting thoughts. But they are not really about anything.'

'We need to restrain our mind. Giving up all desires except uncovering what you are, which is your happiness, includes restraining the mind by restraining speaking and action. Stopping these activities leads to Self Knowledge. So solitude is your friend.

To have solitude you don't have to be alone, you just have to be detached from the world. To restrain your speech doesn't mean you can't speak, just that you are not inclined to. To restrain actions doesn't mean you can't do things, it is just that you are not inclined to because you want to stay with your inner happiness.'

◎

When the man in Khaki had gone, the boy closed his eyes and followed what the man had suggested. He continued walking his path. He sat in stillness for hours every day.

After many days in the same rest house, the boy decided to move on and walk back on the road. He had not seen the man in khaki since he told him about staying in the present and now he wanted his help again.

He had spent much of every day looking at what he was and what he was not, both with his eyes closed and with his eyes open.

He now saw that he was at another block in finding out what he was. He felt he was not finding out about his inner self and so he went back on the road to see if he would meet up with the man.

He set off walking in the early morning warmth and by the middle of the afternoon he was sitting in the third rest house of the day.

He sat with closed eyes using the sound the man had given him to make thoughts less frequent until there were some moments without them. During these brief moments he felt a deep peace.

He was brought to open his eyes by the sense that the man was sitting on the end of the wooden bench, which he was.

After a long time, the man turned to look at him. They exchanged an almost identical smile as they sat in silence.

The old man was calm and sat quite still as he looked out from the table onto the road outside. His mind was free of thoughts as he stared straight ahead. He was not concerned about the future. He was not concerned about anything. He was minding his own business and detached from everything in the outside world. He was as happy as he could be as he sat smiling, looking straight ahead onto the road outside.

The boy broke the long silence.

'I am still getting thoughts. But again, they are not really about anything. They disturb the calmness I have found.'

'The calmness we find inside is stillness. It is our stillness. It is our very self.

It is not possible to use words to describe it because everything about it is beyond words because it is our consciousness.

When you look at a great mountain, one of the most impressive things about it is not its size. The most impressive thing about a great mountain is not its height. What affects us the most is its stillness.

When you look at the stars in the sky, you see it is us who are moving. They are still. Stillness is your nature too and that is what your calmness is.'

◎

When the man in Khaki had gone, the boy closed his eyes and followed what the man had suggested. He continued walking his path. He sat in stillness for hours every day.

After many days in the same rest house, the boy decided to move on and walk back on the road. He had not seen the man in khaki since he told him about restraining the mind and now he wanted his help again.

He had spent much of every day looking at what he was and what he was not, both with his eyes closed and with his eyes open.

He now saw that he was at another block in finding out what he was. He felt he was not finding out about his inner self and so he went back on the road to see if he would meet up with the man.

He set off walking in the early morning warmth and by the middle of the afternoon he was sitting in the third rest house of the day.

He sat with closed eyes using the sound the man had given him to make thoughts less frequent until there were some moments without them. During these brief moments he felt a deep peace.

He was brought to open his eyes by the sense that the man was sitting on the end of the wooden bench, which he was.

After a long time, the man turned to look at him. They exchanged an almost identical smile as they sat in silence.

The old man was calm and sat quite still as he looked out from the table onto the road outside. His mind was free of thoughts as he stared straight ahead. He was not concerned about the future. He was not concerned about anything. He was minding his own business and detached from everything in the outside world. He was as happy as he could be as he sat smiling, looking straight ahead onto the road outside.

The boy broke the long silence.

'I want to know more about consciousness.'

'The ancients used to say different things about it such as, I am That, or That thou art or Be still and know that I am God.

Essentially All is one, All is one self and One is all.

Unfortunately, the scriptures broadcast this out to everyone in the hope that people will just believe it. Of course it is possible to blindly believe, but it is not knowing. Knowing can only be achieved by finding out for yourself, by yourself. All and self are no different. One is All.

◎

When the man in Khaki had gone, the boy closed his eyes and followed what the man had suggested. He continued walking his path. He sat in stillness for hours every day.

After many days in the same rest house, the boy decided to move on and walk back on the road. He had not seen the man in khaki since he told him about consciousness and one is all. He wanted his help again.

He had spent much of every day looking at what he was and what he was not, both with his eyes closed and with his eyes open.

He now saw that he was at another block in finding out what he was. He felt he was not finding out about his inner self and so he went back on the road to see if he would meet up with the man.

He set off walking in the early morning warmth and by the middle of the afternoon he was sitting in the third rest house of the day.

He sat with closed eyes using the sound the man had given him to make thoughts less frequent until there were some moments without them. During these brief moments he felt a deep peace.

He was brought to open his eyes by the sense that the man was sitting on the end of the wooden bench, which he was.

After a long time, the man turned to look at him. They exchanged an almost identical smile as they sat in silence.

The old man was calm and sat quite still as he looked out from the table onto the road outside. His mind was free of thoughts as he stared straight ahead. He was not concerned about the future. He was not concerned about anything. He was minding his own business and detached from everything in the outside world. He was as happy as he could be as he sat smiling, looking straight ahead onto the road outside.

The boy broke the long silence.

'I want to know more about what you said about consciousness and One is All.'

'Consciousness is realising that we are one with everything in the Universe. We see we are what we conjure up inside our self as God and we see that we are no different from God. The consciousness of what we see as 'I am' is what we are. Eventually we see that All is one and All is one self. All and self are no different.

Being conscious of this all the time is freedom from suffering and is happiness.

We are not suffering. We are not decay and death. We are this consciousness. We are this consciousness of stillness which is happiness.

To have seen this, you will have to have meditated until the world of individuals appears as a dream. You see you and you see all is one.

To be your self, all you need to know and be is the 'that' of 'Thou art that.'

◎

When the man in Khaki had gone, the boy closed his eyes and followed what the man had suggested. He continued walking his path. He sat in stillness for hours every day.

After many days in the same rest house, the boy decided to move on and walk back on the road. He had not seen the man in khaki since he told him about consciousness and seeing the dream. He wanted his help again.

He had spent much of every day looking at what he was and what he was not, both with his eyes closed and with his eyes open.

He now saw that he was at another block in finding out what he was. He felt he was not finding out about his inner self and so he went back on the road to see if he would meet up with the man.

He set off walking in the early morning warmth and by the middle of the afternoon he was sitting in the third rest house of the day.

He sat with closed eyes using the sound the man had given him to make thoughts less frequent until there were some moments without them. During these brief moments he felt a deep peace.

He was brought to open his eyes by the sense that the man was sitting on the end of the wooden bench, which he was.

After a long time, the man turned to look at him. They exchanged an almost identical smile as they sat in silence.

The old man was calm and sat quite still as he looked out from the table onto the road outside. His mind was free of thoughts as he stared straight ahead. He was not concerned about the future. He was not concerned about anything. He was minding his own business and detached from everything in the outside world. He was as happy as he could be as he sat smiling, looking straight ahead onto the road outside.

The boy broke the long silence.

'I want to know more about meditation and consciousness.'

'Meditation brings you to one pointedness of your consciousness. You see there is no division between consciousness in meditation and consciousness when your eyes are open.

The world of individuals appears as a dream. You see all is one. You see there is no division. You are that. We are only distracted by our thoughts.

You see that you are the witness. This consciousness becomes the lens through which you see everything.

Giving up the world as we have seen it, giving up thoughts, giving up the body as we have seen it and giving up all scriptures lets us see and know 'all is one self,' so we can just be it.'

◎

When the man in Khaki had gone, the boy closed his eyes and followed what the man had suggested. He continued walking his path. He sat in stillness for hours every day.

After many days in the same rest house, the boy decided to move on and walk back on the road. He had not seen the man in khaki since he told him about consciousness and seeing the dream. He wanted his help again.

He had spent much of every day looking at what he was and what he was not, both with his eyes closed and with his eyes open.

He now saw that he was at another block in finding out what he was. He felt he was not finding out about his inner self and so he went back on the road to see if he would meet up with the man.

He set off walking in the early morning warmth and by the middle of the afternoon he was sitting in the third rest house of the day.

He sat with closed eyes using the sound the man had given him to make thoughts less frequent until there were some moments without them. During these brief moments he felt a deep peace.

He was brought to open his eyes by the sense that the man was sitting on the end of the wooden bench, which he was.

After a long time, the man turned to look at him. They exchanged an almost identical smile as they sat in silence.

The old man was calm and sat quite still as he looked out from the table onto the road outside. His mind was free of thoughts as he stared straight ahead. He was not concerned about the future. He was not concerned about anything. He was minding his own business and detached

from everything in the outside world. He was as happy as he could be as he sat smiling, looking straight ahead onto the road outside.

The boy broke the long silence.

'I want to know more about being still.'

'Always remember that giving up the world as we have seen it, giving up thoughts, giving up the body as we have seen it and giving up all scriptures lets us see and know all is one self, so we can just be it.'

'How do I know when I have done this?'

'There is no such thing as having done it because that is in the past. You have to always be doing it.

But since you ask, perfection is when we don't see our Self as the body. Perfection is when we don't look for any enjoyment outside. Perfection is when our thoughts don't turn outside.' When he said this he looked at the boy, smiled, slowly raised himself up and left.

◎

When the man in Khaki had gone, the boy closed his eyes and followed what the man had suggested. He continued walking his path. He sat in stillness for hours every day.

After many days in the same rest house, the boy decided to move on and walk back on the road. He had not seen the man in khaki since he told him about consciousness and one is all and all is one. He wanted his help again.

He had spent much of every day looking at what he was and what he was not, both with his eyes closed and with his eyes open.

He now saw that he was at another block in finding out what he was. He felt he was not finding out about his inner self and so he went back on the road to see if he would meet up with the man.

He set off walking in the early morning warmth and by the middle of the afternoon he was sitting in the third rest house of the day.

He sat with closed eyes using the sound the man had given him to make thoughts less frequent until there were some moments without them. During these brief moments he felt a deep peace.

He was brought to open his eyes by the sense that the man was sitting on the end of the wooden bench, which he was.

After a long time, the man turned to look at him. They exchanged an almost identical smile as they sat in silence.

The old man was calm and sat quite still as he looked out from the table onto the road outside. His mind was free of thoughts as he stared straight ahead. He was not concerned about the future. He was not concerned about anything. He was minding his own business and detached from everything in the outside world. He was as happy as he could be as he sat smiling, looking straight ahead onto the road outside.

The boy broke the long silence.

'I want to know more about giving up what is outside and what is inside.'

Giving up the world as we have seen it, giving up thoughts as we saw them, giving up the body as we have seen it and giving up all scriptures lets us see and know 'all is one self,' so we can just be it.

But it is not giving up anything at all. Nothing is lost. Nothing is gained. It is simply uncovering what we can't see about it. It is removing our ignorance about it. It is removing the darkness in us by lighting up what is there and seeing what we are. It is not adding something or removing something. It is simply seeing what is here.

◎

When the man in Khaki had gone, the boy closed his eyes and followed what the man had suggested. He continued walking his path. He sat in stillness for hours every day.

After many days in the same rest house, the boy decided to move on and walk back on the road. He had not seen the man in khaki since he told him about consciousness and one is all and all is one. He wanted his help again.

He had spent much of every day looking at what he was and what he was not, both with his eyes closed and with his eyes open.

He now saw that he was at another block in finding out what he was.

He felt he was not finding out about his inner self and so he went back on the road to see if he would meet up with the man.

He set off walking in the early morning warmth and by the middle of the afternoon he was sitting in the third rest house of the day.

He sat with closed eyes using the sound the man had given him to make thoughts less frequent until there were some moments without them. During these brief moments he felt a deep peace.

He was brought to open his eyes by the sense that the man was sitting on the end of the wooden bench, which he was.

After a long time, the man turned to look at him. They exchanged an almost identical smile as they sat in silence.

The old man was calm and sat quite still as he looked

out from the table onto the road outside. His mind was free of thoughts as he stared straight ahead. He was not concerned about the future. He was not concerned about anything. He was minding his own business and detached from everything in the outside world. He was as happy as he could be as he sat smiling, looking straight ahead onto the road outside.

The boy broke the long silence.

'How are you at peace with everything?'

'When we remove our ignorance, we see how nature works. We also see that we if we accept what is in front of us without wanting to change it, we set up less resistance.

If we do everything without trying so hard. If we do everything without wanting results, progress happens more easily and more naturally.

◎

When the man in Khaki had gone, the boy closed his eyes and followed what the man had suggested. He continued walking his path. He sat in stillness for hours every day.

After many days in the same rest house, the boy decided to move on and walk back on the road. He had not seen the man in khaki since he told him about giving up struggling. He wondered when he would see him again.

He had spent much of every day looking at what he was and what he was not, both with his eyes closed and with his eyes open.

He now saw that he was at another block in finding out what he was. He felt he was not finding out about his inner self and so he went back on the road to see if he would meet up with the man.

He set off walking in the early morning warmth and

138

by the middle of the afternoon he was sitting in the third rest house of the day.

He sat with closed eyes using the sound the man had given him to make thoughts less frequent until there were some moments without them. During these moments he felt a deep peace . . .

. . . The boy's deep peace was slowly brought to a close by the sense that someone was sitting on the end of the wooden bench, which he was sitting on. They looked familiar. As he turned to look at the person, he looked at his own arms and noticed that the hairs were all grey. His skin was wrinkled and he was wearing baggy khaki trousers and a khaki shirt. He smiled and nodded at the boy sitting on the other end of the bench.

A single tear ran from the corner of each eye down each cheek, which he quickly wiped. He saw that he was no longer a boy.

The young boy noticed how happy this stranger seemed, even though he was old and on his own. He wondered for a while how anyone could be so happy.

When the man smiled at the boy and nodded, the boy noticed him wiping a tear from either eye.

There was no conversation as neither talked. The boy's head was full of concerns about his future. His eyes looked this way and then the other way. He was a little fidgety and not particularly calm. He was not concerned with the old man.

As the young boy thought about the next part of his walking, he realised how tired he was. He was worried he would never find a home and this made him worry that he would never be happy.

139

The old man was calm and sat quite still as he looked out from the table onto the road outside. His mind was free of thoughts as he stared straight ahead. He was not concerned about the future. He was not concerned about anything. He was minding his own business and detached from everything. He was as happy as he could be as he sat smiling, looking straight ahead onto the road outside.

◎

After two hours of walking, the heat from the bright hot midday sun forced the boy to find more water. He saw a similar sheltered building in the distance and quickened his pace in anticipation of quenching his thirst.

Like the previous building, it was dark but he found a long wooden bench behind a table facing the road and sat down. As his eyes adjusted from the bright sunlight to the unlit coolness of the building, he saw that the man from his previous stop had got there before him and was sitting on the end of his bench.

There was no conversation as neither talked. The boy's head was full of concerns about his future. His eyes looked this way and then the other way. He was a little fidgety and not particularly calm. He was not concerned with the old man.

As he thought about the next part of his walking, he realised how tired he was. He was worried he would never find a home and this made him worry that he would never be happy.

The old man was calm and sat quite still as he looked out from the table onto the road outside. His mind was free of thoughts as he stared straight ahead. He was not concerned about the future. He was not concerned about anything. He was minding his own business and detached

from everything in the outside world. He was as happy as he could be as he sat smiling, looking straight ahead onto the road outside.

The boy noticed again how happy this stranger seemed, even though he was old and on his own. He wondered for a while how anyone could be so happy and he realised he didn't have any answers to how he could be as happy.

After some time the man felt rested and straightened his skinny legs, rose from the bench and left. The boy sat looking ahead at the road for some time. He finished his cool drink and realised it was past midday. He thought he should begin walking on the hot dusty road again to make progress.

◎

After two hours of walking, the heat from the bright hot early afternoon sun forced the boy to find more water. He saw a similar sheltered building in the distance and quickened his pace in anticipation of quenching his thirst.

Like the previous building it was dark but he found a long wooden bench behind a table facing the road and sat down. As his eyes adjusted from the bright sunlight to the unlit coolness of the building, once again he saw that the man from his previous stop had got there before him and was sitting on the end of his bench.

There was no conversation as neither talked. The boy's head was full of concerns about his future. His eyes looked this way and then the other way. He was a little fidgety and not particularly calm. He was not concerned with the old man.

As he thought about the next part of his walking, he realised how tired he was. He was worried he would never

141

find a home and this made him worry that he would never be happy.

The old man was calm and sat quite still as he looked out from the table onto the road outside. His mind was free of thoughts as he stared straight ahead. He was not concerned about the future. He was not concerned about anything. He was minding his own business and detached from everything in the outside world. He was as happy as he could be as he sat smiling, looking straight ahead onto the road outside.

The boy noticed again how happy this stranger seemed, even though he was old and on his own. He wondered for a while how anyone could be so happy and once again he realised he didn't have any answers to how he could be as happy.

But he was also curious and even though he was a little reluctant to strike up conversations with strangers, he asked the man.

'How come you seem so happy?'

'I am happy because I work hard just to be happy.' He looked at the boy then looked straight ahead. After some time the man felt rested and straightened his skinny legs, rose from the bench and left.

The boy started wondering if he would ever be that happy. He wanted that more than anything else he could think of.

◎

After two hours of walking, the heat from the bright hot late afternoon sun forced him to find more water. He saw a similar sheltered building in the distance and quickened his pace in anticipation of quenching his thirst.

Like the previous building, it was dark but he found

a long wooden bench behind a table facing the road and sat down. As his eyes adjusted from the bright sunlight to the unlit coolness of the building, once again he saw that the man from his previous stop had got there before him and was sitting on the end of his bench.

There was no conversation as neither talked. The boy's head was full of concerns about his future. His eyes looked this way and then the other way. He was a little fidgety and not particularly calm. He was not concerned with the old man.

As he thought about the next part of his walking, he realised how tired he was. He was worried he would never find a home and this made him worry that he would never be happy.

The old man was calm and sat quite still as he looked out from the table onto the road outside. His mind was free of thoughts as he stared straight ahead. He was not concerned about the future. He was not concerned about anything. He was minding his own business and detached from everything in the outside world. He was as happy as he could be as he sat smiling, looking straight ahead onto the road outside.

The boy noticed again how happy this stranger seemed, even though he was old and on his own. He wondered for a while how anyone could be so happy and once again he realised he didn't have any answers to how he could be as happy.

'I saw you walking in front me. How did you get here so much before me?'

'I saw you walking behind me. I knew you were already following my path. I don't mean the actual physical path you take when you are walking, even though it seems that way. You are about to follow the path in life I took.'

'How do you know that?'

'I have been where you are now going. I did it in the past and you will do it in the future. But we are both here now. Whichever way you go, you will be following me. So, I will be there with you.'

∞

4.

The Cave

Like Groundhog Day, it can seem that repeated effort keeps on returning us to the same place. But with perseverance, eventually we see who we are.

The young man and the young woman had put off all plans for the future to make this journey. The aim was to find out about a man who lived on a hill. There was something about him which was different.

Neither Lily nor Conor had found happiness. They had found many overlapping clues and were now searching for the answer here in a small town in South India.

Lily's ability to judge things well, to discuss and argue down to the smallest detail made her teachers think that one day she could be someone as powerful and as important as a judge.

This was encouraged by Lily's parents who had adopted her at six weeks from a twenty one year old woman, whose fiance had left her for someone else. Instead, Lily shunned people who had power and seemed important and found those with humility the most interesting and best teachers.

Although Lily knew the language and intricacies of small talk, it was not for her and so she avoided it. She was polite and although she was kind when any opportunity arose, she was detached from the world. Because of this she did not fit in. Other than necessary discussion, she appeared private and quiet, as if impenetrable. She was described as a serious person.

Conor had almost continuous periods of solitude which could last for several days. Although his mood was cheerful and positive, he was so withdrawn he would hardly speak all day. Then he would have a brief release from what he had been churning over.

It was often a question he had raised about happiness. Sometimes it was about what he didn't want to do next, because unlike most young men in their late twenties, he could not stay in one job with the same people for longer than a few months.

Unlike his unpredictable father, a war veteran, whose sense of anything spiritual or worthwhile, came from the effects of bottles of spirits, Conor was sensitive, turned inwards and positive. His father was either absent or abusive.

Conor was not able to talk about the things he wanted to with other young men because they showed little or no interest in the inner workings of people. He was not just bored by their obsessional talk about securities in the material world, he could no longer tolerate it. He could not put up with listening to anyone who wanted to talk passionately about the value of their house, the latest investment, their next promotion or how big their pension pot was. He had no interest in securities of that kind. Instead, Conor was interested in what could make him happy from inside.

He was more curious than Lily about other people's inner lives and would often describe to Lily how someone could simplify and untangle a complicated situation they had got into. Sometimes Lily's only way to end Conor's occasional chatter was to stand up, turn around and pretend she was busy looking for something.

Unlike Lily, Conor would not politely excuse himself from people he didn't want to listen to. He would quietly leave without saying anything. His detachment from the things of the world also made him not fit in. He was seen as someone who had his values the wrong way around, who lived in another world. Not someone of the real world.

They had looked for answers in books. They had received advice and guidance from well-meaning and not so well-meaning people who were supposed to help and heal but nothing had helped heal what seemed like a missing part of them.

148

They had known each other since college and had agreed to be friends. Although both were seriously committed to being single, they had agreed to travel together several times. They were here searching for happiness.

They agreed this small South Indian town had something different about it. It seemed like their most solemn time together. It was as if something was going to happen to them. Because of this, there was a different quality of silence between them, which neither mentioned.

The man they were looking for had lived in a cave on this hill for many years. On the lower slopes of this hill was a town which had been built around an ancient temple. It was known that he chose to live on the hill because it was regarded as a sacred mountain. They knew that he rarely spoke and what could be learnt from him was usually received in silence. To them, although this was against rational thinking, it seemed as if it had the authority of truth because they both had a sense that truth didn't have any words to describe it.

◎

At the foot of the hill, they looked around for somewhere to stay but could not identify any guest houses. Lily stopped a man who was walking slowly in front of them.

'Do you know a guest house we can stay in for the night?'

'How long are you staying?'

'Just a night or two. We have come to see the man on the hill.' Lily answered.

'There is a guest room just a few yards from here. The person who owns it lets visitors to the cave stay without any charge. Look, it is just over there on the left.'

He walked ahead to a gate which he opened. A path led to a clearing in front of a small house. He walked to the side of the house where he opened a wooden side door for them. He then walked back down the path through the gate.

'Thank you.' Conor said as he turned and looked over the other side of the gate, but the man was gone.

'This is good but maybe it's also disappointing.' Lily said.

'How do you mean?' Asked Conor.

'Well, if the owner lets people stay here free of charge, it must mean visitors probably don't stay long at all, or there are not many visitors. It may not bode well for our visit.'

'You know we are different. We both come from suffering. We are strange. Maybe we will stay longer than others have. Let's just see.'

An hour later they had changed, drunk some water and were ready to find the cave. They set off walking clockwise around the hill but couldn't make out any obvious worn area like a path. Conor noticed the man who had shown them to the guest house. He was sitting in the shade of a rock beside the road. Conor approached him.

'You kindly showed us the guest room.'

'I have not forgotten you already.'

'Do you know the best way up the hill to the cave?'

'There are several ways up to the cave. The direct one is just a little ahead. You will see a path off the road going to the right. It's a simple walk, gentle at first then a little steeper for a few more minutes. Then it is a steady climb which takes effort.

'How will we know when we are there?' Conor asked.

'You'll come to a large lighter coloured rock ahead of you. There is a small clearing in front of it. Over the years various people have dug out the earth beneath the centre of the rock above, so it is now a cave. There are a few attendants up there who look after everyone's needs. Very few people visit the cave.'

'Is there a reason for that?' Lily asked.

'Most people want something else, a wish fulfilled, prayers answered or blessings, that sort of thing. Most people don't want his kind of instruction in silence. It's unusual for people to want to look inside.'

'I hear what you say.' Lily acknowledged.

'I see from your clothes you have travelled a long way to get here.'

'We feel this is where we are supposed to be.'

'Few people come here and almost no one stays. They go back to their lives after a day or two.'

'Does anyone stay?'

'It is unusual.' He paused and looked up the hill, then looked at them. 'The ones who stay have endured enough suffering.'

'You don't mean people come here to die? Lily asked.

'They come here to live fully. They have turned away from what most people want.'

'So, their old life is over?'

'Yes. The ones who stay, stay forever.' He noticed their direct firm gaze into his eyes drop to the ground. 'I see you are placing a lot in this man.'

'Yes.' Lily said, looking back up at the hill. They were silent for some time looking up at the hill. Then Lily, reconnecting her gaze with the man added, 'We have travelled searching but something has been calling from inside. Something is calling from inside to be here now.'

'I'm always around this place, so if you need help let me know. It's wise to take up some food and water with

151

you for you and the attendants. You never know how long you will be.'

◎

They replaced the stores of food and water in the packs they carried on their backs, with more for the attendants, just as the man had suggested.

Soon after, they were taking one slow small step at a time up the hill.

'He said it would be a little steeper for a few minutes but we've been walking up for forty-five minutes now.' As she said this, Conor stopped.

'This direct way he said is simple but hard work. I need to stop to rest for a few moments.'

They stopped and climbed up on top of a boulder and sat down. There were hundreds of these boulders of all shapes and sizes which seemed like they had been scattered randomly all over the whole hill.

They sat looking around the hill. They looked down the hill at the town. They looked up the hill, then they looked at each other. There was a smile which they gave each other, expressing compassion and friendship. Again, they looked down at the town and then Lily closed her eyes and said softly, 'We are here after a very long journey.'

Conor closed his eyes and said in a low voice, 'We are home. I hope at last we're going to find happiness.'

'We are where we want to be.' Lily said softly, still with her eyes closed. They sat and got their breath back from the climb.

'This could be the place. Look ahead.' Conor said. 'There's a large rock which looks a bit lighter than the others around here.'

'You're right.' Lily said as she slid down the boulder

and sprung up a couple of steps ahead of Connor. 'It looks like there's a clearing in front of it.'

As she approached the clearing, she noticed the entrance was about twenty feet across and about ten feet high.

Two men came towards them from inside the cave. The men moved apart from each other and stood either side to let them pass. The two men looked at them, then bowed their heads in a respectful way. The man on the left beckoned with his upturned hand for them to enter the cave. Lily bent down to remove her sandals and seeing this, Conor bent down and removed his also. They were slightly nervous about entering the cave but at the same time they sensed being welcome.

Conor led the way slowly and carefully forwards. After a short walk he could see the figure of someone sitting on the dusty floor of the cave. They were sitting in the position of someone meditating with their legs crossed. Then he could see it was a young man sitting against the wall.

◎

As his eyes accommodated to the darkness, he could make out the young man was about the same age as him. The young man looked peaceful. They stood and looked at the young man for some time.

Conor felt a hand on his shoulder and so he turned to look at Lily. She was pointing ahead into what looked like darkness to him. She took her hand off his shoulder and took a step past him.

Lily led the way slowly and carefully forwards. She could see the figure of someone sitting on the dusty floor of the cave. They were also sitting in the position of someone meditating with their legs crossed. Then she could see it was a young woman sitting against the wall. As her eyes accommodated to the darkness, she could make out the young woman was about the same age as her. The young woman looked peaceful and happy. They stood and looked at the young woman for some time.

Lily felt a hand on her shoulder and so she turned to look at Conor. He was pointing ahead into what looked like darkness to her. He took his hand off her shoulder and took a step past her.

Conor led the way slowly and carefully forwards. He could see the figure of someone sitting on the dusty floor of the cave. Just like the two people before, they were sitting in the position of someone meditating with their legs crossed. Then he could see it was someone sitting against the wall.

As his eyes accommodated to the darkness, he could make out it was a man a bit older than him. The man seemed not only peaceful like the young man before, but he had a smile of happiness. They stood and looked at the man for some time.

Once again, Conor felt Lily's hand on his shoulder and so he turned to look at her. Again, she was pointing ahead into what looked like darkness to him. She slowly took her hand off his shoulder and took a step past him.

Lily led the way slowly and carefully forwards. She could see the figure of someone sitting on the dusty floor of the cave. Just like the young woman before, they were sitting in the position of someone meditating with their legs crossed. Then she could see it was someone sitting against the wall.

As her eyes accommodated to the darkness, she could make out it was a woman a bit older than her. She noticed at once that the other woman seemed serene and happy. Lily stood and looked at her for some time.

154

Conor caught up with her and stood beside her in silence at this fourth seated figure sitting cross legged with their eyes closed.

◎

They walked side by side slowly along the cave. The natural light from the entrance had long ago faded and had been replaced by light from simple lamps. Every ten steps or so there was a stone which had a hollow carved out on the top. In the hollow at the top of each stone was a small wick, alight from the oil it was laying in.

As they walked along the cave, the dim light didn't light enough of the cave for them to see and feel their footings easily. They looked at each other and looked back towards the entrance, then at each other again. They had both made the same decision in silence not to carry on walking into the cave.

The way back to the entrance of the cave seemed much shorter than the way into the cave.

Once outside the cave, their eyes squinted at the bright daylight.

They sat down in the clearing outside the entrance to the cave to reflect and to quench their thirst. They shared a bottle of water and gave the other one to one of the attendants. They got out their food supply for the day but only ate a little before deciding to climb down the hill. They wondered if the attendants would like the remaining food, so they offered it to the attendants who accepted it with a nod of gratitude.

'It was so still,' Lily said. 'I felt I wanted break the silence and ask them a question. I wanted to ask how I could be as happy as they are.'

'Yes, me too. I wanted to ask them that as well, but I

didn't want to break the peace. It was so peaceful there. It was so still, I could feel me moving the air as I walked into the cave.'

They were surprised to see that the sun was now on the other side of the hill and was going to start to set on the horizon soon. They began their walk down the hill. This seemed to take a much shorter time than they had expected.

They had an early evening meal of vegetables and fruit from a nearby stall and slept soundly in their room.

◎

It was two hours before dawn when Lily and Conor woke up. Without any hesitation, they got on with their only task of the day. They were going up the hill to find out more about the man from the people in the cave.

On the way to the path up the mountain, they bought some more water and extra provisions. On the way back to the path up the mountain, again they noticed the man who had shown them guest room. He was walking in front of them. Not wanting to disturb him again, they walked slowly behind him at a distance until they came to the path up the mountain. He walked past the path but just before they turned up the mountain path, he turned around, stopped and looked at them with a peaceful smile, nodding his head, as if in a knowing, approving way.

The way up the mountain seemed different. They noticed more this time. The many massive boulders were scattered all around as if they had been thrown from the top. As they slowly walked up between the rocks, they saw how much vegetation they had missed seeing before.

A third of the way up the hill there were some tall palm trees in an area where there was a spring. This made the area look like an oasis in the tropics. They had also overlooked that there were cacti from two to twelve feet high on much of the lower slopes of the hill.

Occasionally they saw someone higher up walking up or down in a different area of the mountain. They both knew that there was something simple and honest about the hill. They felt it was trying to show them something they were not able to put into words.

When they reached the opening of the cave, the two attendants came towards them from inside the cave. They moved apart from each other, standing either side to let them pass, bowing their heads in a respectful way. The man on the left recognised them and smiled, beckoned with his upturned hand for them to enter the cave.

They walked into the cave, noticing more this time the light from the cave entrance being replaced by light from the simple oil lamps on top of rocks. They came to where the young man who they had seen before had been but he was gone.

A little further they came to where the young woman they had also seen had been sitting. She was also gone. The attendant beckoned them to walk on.

As they continued walking into the cave, the light from the simple oil lamps on top of rocks seemed like guiding beacons. Eventually they came to the older man and woman who they had seen before.

The attendant beckoned Lily to sit in front of the woman who was sitting on the dusty floor of the cave. She was sitting against the wall of the cave in the position of someone meditating with her legs crossed.

◎

Lily accepted the invitation and sat several feet away with

157

her back leaning against the opposite wall of the cave. She sat with the woman and closed her eyes.

The attendant then beckoned Conor to sit in front of the man who was sitting on the dusty floor of the cave. He was sitting against the wall of the cave in the position of someone meditating with his legs crossed.

Conor accepted the invitation and sat several feet away with his back leaning against the opposite wall of the cave. He sat with the man and closed his eyes.

After some time, the visitors opened their eyes when they heard the man and woman opposite them making sounds of movements.

The two visitors looked at the man and woman. It was as if there was an unspoken warmness of shared purpose between them. The first to speak was Lily.

'Can you help by telling me how I can sit and be happy like you?'

There was a long silence whilst words were found to express the answer. The woman spoke slowly with long pauses between her words.

∞

'There is no mystery.'

∞

'It is simple.'

∞

'It is mind control.'

∞

158

'The mind comes up with thoughts almost all the time.'

∞

'Without thoughts there is stillness. This is what we all look for to be happy.'

∞

'Some can simply experience this stillness when they close their eyes. But most of us can't.'

∞

'Stillness can't be experienced easily because thoughts keep on interrupting our natural stillness.'

∞

'Our inner stillness can only be experienced by making effort to keep thoughts away.'

∞

'Whether you use a sound at first or not does not matter as long as you keep thoughts away.'

∞

'But at first most of us need the help of a sound to repeat to see what inner stillness can be without thoughts.'

∞

'To the mind, the sound is just like the rope you use to tether an animal to one place, otherwise it would wander off.'

∞

'We start by repeating a sound quietly inside, but we soon drift off thinking and forget to repeat the sound.'

∞

'Coming back to the sound shows how thoughts interrupt the experience of simply repeating a sound.'

∞

'Repeatedly returning to the sound shows the constant coming of thoughts.'

∞

'Thoughts are seen for what they are and what they do to our natural inner stillness.' She looked to the man to her side, who spoke as slowly with long pauses between his words.

∞

'It is simple.'

∞

'You use a sound like a tool to show you how your

160

thoughts intrude on your inner stillness.'

∞

'It is usually a temporary tool.' he said, gesturing for the woman beside him to continue.

∞

'The sound is repeated at first slowly, aloud. Then repeated more and more quietly. Then quieter until it is repeated only silently inside.'

∞

'Thoughts always compete with the repeating sound and overwhelm the sound. So, we have to bring the sound back to the front of our consciousness.'

∞

'Can you show us?' Conor asked.

∞

'When you come back here, I will show you.' Said the man.

∞

After he said this, he turned away from the visitors and he beckoned the woman to follow him back into the cave. They turned around to smile at the visitors and a few moments later they disappeared back into the cave.

161

After some time, Lily and Conor got up to return to the outside. They stood up and both felt that they were deep inside the cave. Again, they began walking back to the entrance of the cave. The way out of the cave again seemed much shorter than the way into the cave.

◎

Once outside the cave, they squinted at the bright day-light. They sat down in the clearing outside the entrance to the cave to quench their thirst. They shared a bottle of water and gave the other one to one of the attendants. After opening their food supply for the day, they only ate a little before deciding to climb down the hill.

Wondering if the attendants would like the remaining food, they offered it to the attendants who accepted it with a nod of gratitude.

'I found that so positive.' Lily said. 'I feel as if a whole load of worrying has been removed from me. It's like I've had a bath inside and somehow all the dirt has gone.'

'I know exactly what you mean by that. Being inside the cave made me feel something which makes me know we are in the right place.' Conor said looking over to her.

'Visiting the cave has taken most of the day.' Lily said, looking to the other side of the hill.

'The sun is going to start to set on the horizon soon.' Conor pointed out.

They began their walk back down the hill. This seemed to take a much shorter time than before.

When they were back down on the road, they noticed the man who had given them directions up the hill and the room. He was walking in front of them. He turned to look at them, smiled and walked on ahead.

On the way to their room, they stopped at a nearby stall. They had an early evening meal of vegetables and fruit from the nearby stall and slept soundly in their room.

◎

They had never experienced heat like the beginning of a typical South Indian Summer. When they woke, even though the sun had not yet risen they were perspiring. Despite the heat, Conor and Lily got on with their only task for the day. They were going up the hill to the cave to find out more.

On the way to the path up the mountain, they bought some more water and extra provisions. On the way back to the path up the mountain, once again they noticed the same man walking in front of them. They did not want to disturb him again, so they walked slowly behind him at a distance until they came to the path up the mountain. He walked past the path but just before they turned up the mountain path, he turned around, stopped and looked at them with a peaceful smile, nodding his head, as if in a knowing, approving way.

Because of the heat, the way up the mountain felt much harder work than before. It was a very slow walk because they could only walk for a short time before having to stop to cool down. They waited each time, resting against boulders until the thumping from their rapid heartbeats subsided.

Occasionally whilst resting under the shade of trees lining the windy path, they noticed that there were trees in abundance on the lower slopes of the mountain which reached almost as high as the pale rock cave they were visiting.

They had thought the mountain was bare of life but slowly as they walked up, they noticed paw prints and began to see that many things lived on it.

Each time after they recovered their breath,
walking slowly up between the boulders, they felt more
relaxed about the man and the people in the cave.

When they reached the opening of the cave, the
two attendants came towards them from inside the cave.
They moved apart from each other, standing either side
to let them pass, bowing their heads in a respectful way.
The man on the left recognised them and smiled, then
beckoned with his upturned hand for them to enter the
cave.

They walked into the cave, noticing more this time
the light from the cave entrance being replaced by light
from the simple oil lamps on top of rocks. They came to
where the young man and woman who they had seen
before had been and walked on.

As they continued walking into the cave, the light
from the simple oil lamps on top of rocks seemed like
guiding beacons. Eventually they came to the woman who
they had seen before and a little further they came to the
man they had also seen.

The attendant beckoned Lily to sit in front of the
woman who was sitting on the dusty floor of the cave. She
was sitting against the wall of the cave in the position of
someone meditating with her legs crossed.

◎

Lily accepted the invitation and sat several feet away with
her back leaning against the opposite wall of the cave. She
closed her eyes and sat with the woman.

The attendant then beckoned Conor to sit in front of
the man who was sitting on the dusty floor of the cave. He
was sitting against the wall of the cave in the position of

someone meditating with his legs crossed.

Conor accepted the invitation and sat several feet away with his back leaning against the opposite wall of the cave. He closed his eyes and sat with the man.

After some time, the visitors opened their eyes when they heard the man and woman opposite them making sounds of movements.

The two visitors looked at the man and woman. It was as if there was an unspoken warmness of shared purpose between them.

The man spoke slowly with long pauses between his words.

∞

'This is a sound you can use.' He said.

∞

He made a two-syllable sound and invited Lily and Conor to repeat it with him. He made the two-syllable sound again, but quieter, suggesting to them that they also say it more quietly. He made the two-syllable sound once again, but even quieter. He repeated this until the sound was so quite it became obvious that it was meant to be said silently and heard only inside.

∞

'Now close your eyes and continue.'

∞

Lily and Conor sat hearing the sound inside whilst

165

both lost their sense of time.

∞

After some time, the young visitors opened their eyes, followed by the young man and woman sitting opposite.

∞

'What now?' Lily asked the young woman.

∞

'Much effort is needed.'

∞

After she said this, she turned away from the visitors and she beckoned the young man to follower her back into the cave. They turned around to smile at the visitors and a few moments later they disappeared back into the cave.

◉

After some time, Lily and Conor got up to return to the outside. They stood up and both felt that they were deep inside the cave. Again, they began walking back to the entrance of the cave. The way out of the cave again seemed much shorter than the way into the cave.

Outside, they squinted at the bright daylight.

They sat down in the clearing outside the entrance to the cave to quench their thirst, shared one bottle of water and gave the other one to one of the attendants.

After opening their food supply for the day, they only ate a little before deciding to climb down the hill.

Wondering if the attendants would like the remaining food, they offered it to the attendants who accepted it with a nod of gratitude.

'I found that so strange. It was like my mind stopped thinking and I was just with me inside myself. I wasn't sure if any thoughts came to me at all.' Lily said.

'I had thoughts coming and going and I had to consciously bring back the sound. My thoughts became much more obvious that they were separate from each other and something different from the sound.' Conor said.

'I feel a bit like I'm floating.' Lily added.

'Me too. I feel a bit funny as if I should be laughing. Maybe it's feeling a bit lightheaded, but I do feel strange. But in a good way.'

'That's exactly the way I feel too.' They both sat looking down the hill at the activity of the people in the town below.

Visiting the cave had taken most of the day but they were still surprised to see that the sun was now on the other side of the hill and was going to start to set on the horizon soon. They began their walk back down the hill. This seemed to take a much shorter time than before.

When they were back down on the road, they noticed the man who had given them directions up the hill and the room. He was walking in front of them. He turned to look at them, smiled and walked on ahead.

Back in their room they sat down and closed their eyes. They brought back the sound to the front of their consciousness, repeating it silently and slowly. They sat repeatedly bringing the sound back to the front of their consciousness as thoughts of everyday things kept springing up in their minds.

They had an early evening meal of vegetables and fruit from a nearby stall and slept soundly in the room they rented.

◎

It was an hour before dawn and they were already perspiring. It was getting hotter. They had never experienced heat like this and they struggled to stay focused.

Despite the heat, Lily and Conor got on with their only task for the day. They were going up the hill to the cave to find out more.

On the way to the path up the mountain, they bought some more water and extra provisions. On the way to the path, once again they noticed the same man walking in front of them. They did not want to disturb him again, so they walked slowly behind him at a distance until they came to the path up the mountain. He walked past the path but just before they turned up the mountain path, he stopped, turned around, looked at them with a tranquil smile and then continued.

The way up the mountain seemed even harder than before. As they slowly walked up between the rocks, they sensed something was different. Slowly they noticed the monkeys hiding behind rocks. They both stopped. One by one, black faced Langur monkeys popped their heads up from behind boulders which they had hidden behind.

Lily and Conor stood and stared at them as the monkeys started to play and leap from one boulder to another. They could see the man and woman were no threat to them, so they came closer to inspect them. They were looking for food and because they couldn't see any,

168

they ran back to behind the boulders they had emerged from.

Feeling more relaxed and rested by stopping to see the monkeys and their playfulness, Lily and Conor continued what was now an arduous hot climb up the hill to the cave.

When they reached the opening of the cave, the two attendants came towards them from inside the cave. They moved apart from each other, standing either side to let them pass, bowing their heads in a respectful way. The man on the left recognised them and smiled, then beckoned with his upturned hand for them to enter the cave.

The cave seemed different, a little more familiar. There was no fear about entering it and instead even more of a feeling of being welcomed home.

They walked into the cave, noticing more this time the light from the cave entrance being replaced by light from the simple oil lamps on top of rocks. They came to where the young man and woman who they had seen before had been and walked on.

As they continued walking into the cave, the light from the simple oil lamps on top of rocks seemed like guiding beacons. Eventually they came to the man who they had seen before and a little further they came to the woman they had also seen.

The attendant beckoned Lily to sit in front of the woman who was sitting on the dusty floor of the cave. She was sitting against the wall of the cave in the position of someone meditating with her legs crossed.

◎

Lily accepted the invitation and sat several feet away with her back leaning against the opposite wall of the cave. She closed her eyes and sat with the woman.

The attendant then beckoned Conor to sit in front of the man who was sitting on the dusty floor of the cave. He was sitting against the wall of the cave in the position of someone meditating with his legs crossed.

Conor accepted the invitation and sat several feet away with his back leaning against the opposite wall of the cave. He closed his eyes and sat with the man.

After some time, the visitors opened their eyes when they heard the man and woman opposite them making sounds of movements.

The two visitors looked at the man and woman. It was as if there was an unspoken warmness of shared purpose between them.

Lily was the first to speak.

'Can you tell me more about how I can sit and be happy?'

There was a long silence whilst words were found to express the answer. The man spoke slowly with long pauses between his words.

∞

'Although you already know, let me remind you of what you have learnt. This is to emphasise its importance.'

∞

'There is no mystery.

∞

'It is simple.'

∞

'It is mind control.' Said the man.

∞

'The mind comes up with thoughts almost all the time. Without thoughts there is stillness.'

∞

'This is what we all look for to be happy.'

∞

'Some can simply experience this stillness when they close their eyes. But most of us can't.'

∞

'It can't be experienced easily because thoughts keep on interrupting our natural stillness.'

∞

'Our inner stillness can only be experienced by making special effort to keep thoughts away.'

∞

'Whether you use a sound at first or not does not matter as long as you keep thoughts away.'

171

∞

'But at first most of us need the help of a sound to repeat to see what inner stillness can be without thoughts.'

∞

'To the mind, the sound is just like the rope you use to tether an animal to one place, otherwise it would wander off.'

∞

'As you will have experienced, you start by repeating a sound quietly inside, but we soon drift off thinking about things and you forget to repeat the sound.'

∞

'Coming back to the sound shows how thoughts interrupt the experience of simply repeating a sound.'

∞

'Repeatedly returning to the sound shows the constant coming of thoughts.'

∞

'Thoughts are seen for what they are and what they do to our natural inner stillness.' She looked at the man to continue.

∞

'It is really simple. You use a sound like a tool to show you how your thoughts intrude on your inner stillness.'

∞

'It is usually a temporary tool.' Said the man, gesturing for the woman to continue.

∞

'The sound is repeated slowly, at first aloud. Then repeated more and more quietly. Then quieter until it is repeated only silently inside.'

∞

'Thoughts always compete with the repeating sound and overwhelm the sound. So, we have to bring the sound back to the front of our consciousness.'

∞

'Yes, we have been doing this for some time now.' Conor said. 'I see how my thoughts interrupt the sound and I have to make an effort to bring the sound back. As a result of doing this I feel more relaxed, calmer. I now see there is more to me. I want to know more about this. Can you show me?'

∞

173

'Most importantly, first you need to have simple mind control.' Said the man.

∞

'You need to be able to keep thoughts away and to focus on one thing.'

∞

'This is mind control. It is effort.'

∞

'When you see how to control the mind, you begin to be more conscious of what you are.'

∞

'You see you are not your mind but something bigger.'

∞

'When you know how to control your mind with meditation, you begin to ask what you are.'

∞

'How do you find out?' Asked Conor.

∞

'You see the Self inside yourself by yourself.'

∞

'You see your nature is stillness.'

∞

'This state of consciousness is happiness.'

∞

'How do you know this?' Conor asked woman.

∞

'We are only novices and have learnt from others.'

∞

After she said this, she turned away from the visitors and she beckoned the man to follower her back into the cave. They turned around to smile at the visitors and a few moments later were gone, back into the cave.

After some time, the visitors got up to return to the outside. Again, the way back to the entrance of the cave seemed much shorter than the way into the cave.

◎

Opening their eyes fully, they squinted at the bright daylight.

They sat down in the clearing outside the entrance to the cave to quench their thirst, shared one bottle of water and gave the other one to one of the attendants.

After opening their food supply for the day, they only ate a little before deciding to climb down the hill.

Wondering if the attendants would like the remaining food, they offered it to the attendants who accepted it with a nod of gratitude.

Visiting the cave had taken most of the day but they were still surprised to see that the sun was now on the other side of the hill and was going to start to set on the horizon soon. They began their walk back down the hill. This seemed to take a much shorter time than before.

When they were back down on the road, they noticed the man who had given them directions up the hill and the room. He was walking in front of them. He turned to look at them, smiled and walked on ahead.

Back in their room they sat down and closed their eyes. Lily quietly said, 'Do you remember he said, the sound is a temporary tool and it doesn't matter if we use a sound or not, just as long as we keep thoughts away?'

'Yes, he was clear about that.'

' Let's try not using the sound to focus our attention. Let's try stopping thoughts as they arise. Let's see if we can be still without the sound.'

They sat for longer than before, repeatedly stopping thoughts bothering them once they had appeared.

'I find it easier than using the sound.' Conor said.

'Me too. Maybe let's stick with this way of not having thoughts.'

'It seems more natural to me.'

'It's one less thing to remember. I can see how the sound helps but it's simpler without it.'

They had an early evening meal of vegetables and fruit from a nearby stall and slept soundly in their room.

◎

They were woken an hour before dawn by the intense heat of an Indian Summer. Because of the heat, everything they did seemed as if it was in slow motion because it was not possible to move quickly. When they set off, the sun had not yet risen but they both got on with their only task for the day. Despite the heat they were going up the hill to the cave to find out more.

On the way to the path up the mountain, they bought some extra water and extra provisions. On the way back to the path, again they noticed the same man walking in front of them. They did not want to disturb him again, so they walked slowly behind him at a distance until they came to the path up the mountain. He walked past the path but just before they turned up the mountain path, he stopped, turned around, looked at them with a serene smile and continued.

Because of the heat the way up the mountain felt even more arduous than before. As they slowly walked up between the boulders, they felt more relaxed about the man and the people in the cave.

When they reached the opening of the cave, the two attendants came towards them from inside the cave. They moved apart from each other, standing either side to let them pass, bowing their heads in a respectful way. The man on the left recognised them and smiled, then beckoned with his upturned hand for them to enter the cave.

There was almost more urgency in going inside the cave now. It was as if no time should be wasted.

They walked into the cave, noticing more this time the light from the cave entrance being replaced by light from the simple oil lamps on top of rocks. They came to where the young man and woman who they had seen before had been and walked on.

As they continued walking into the cave, the light from the simple oil lamps on top of rocks seemed like guiding beacons. Eventually they came to the man who they had seen before and a little further they came to the woman they had also seen.

The attendant beckoned Lily to sit in front of the woman who was sitting on the dusty floor of the cave. She was sitting against the wall of the cave in the position of someone meditating with her legs crossed.

◎

Lily accepted the invitation and sat several feet away with her back leaning against the opposite wall of the cave. She closed her eyes and sat with the woman.

The attendant then beckoned Conor to sit in front of the man who was sitting on the dusty floor of the cave. He was sitting against the wall of the cave in the position of someone meditating with his legs crossed.

Conor accepted the invitation and sat several feet away with his back leaning against the opposite wall of the cave. He closed his eyes and sat with the man.

After some time, the visitors opened their eyes when they heard the man and woman opposite them making sounds of movements.

The two visitors looked at the man and woman. It was as if there was an unspoken warmness of shared purpose between them.

Lily was the first to speak.

'I now see there is more to this. I want to know more about this. Can you show me?'

There was a long silence whilst words were found to express the answer. The man spoke slowly with long pauses between his words.

∞

'Most importantly, first you need to have simple mind control.' Said the older man.

∞

'You need to be able to keep thoughts away and to focus on one thing.'

∞

'This is mind control. It is effort.'

∞

'When you see how to control the mind, you begin to be more conscious of what you are.'

∞

'You see you are not your mind but something different.'

∞

'When you know how to control your mind with meditation, you begin to ask what you are.'

∞

'How do you find out?' Conor asked.

179

∞

'You see the Self inside yourself by yourself.'

∞

'You see your nature is stillness.'

∞

'This state of consciousness is happiness.'

∞

'How do you see this?' Lily asked.

∞

'Our difficulty is seeing how simple it is.'

∞

'We are taught and conditioned by the world that we can be happy if we acquire all the things on offer, from material things to knowledge and power.'

∞

'When we see none of these make us happy, but lead to suffering, we start to unveil our inner self, and our ignorance of our true inner self is removed.''

∞

'How do you know this?' Lily asked the older woman.

∞

'We are only novices and have learnt from others.'

∞

After she said this, she turned away from the visitors and she beckoned the man to follower her back into the cave. They turned around to smile at the visitors and a few moments later were gone, back into the cave.

After some time, they got up to return to the outside. Again, the way back to the entrance of the cave seemed much shorter than the way into the cave.

◎

Once outside the cave, Conor and Lily opened their eyes fully and squinted at the bright daylight.

They sat down in the clearing outside the entrance to the cave to quench their thirst, shared one bottle of water and gave the other one to one of the attendants.

After opening their food supply for the day, they only ate a little before deciding to climb down the hill.

Wondering if the attendants would like the remaining food, they offered it to the attendants who accepted it with a nod of gratitude.

Visiting the cave had taken most of the day but they were still surprised to see that the sun was now on the other side of the hill and was going to start to set on the horizon soon. They began their walk back down the hill. This seemed to take a much shorter time than before.

When they were back down on the road, they noticed the man who had given them directions up the hill and the room. He was walking in front of them. He turned to look at them, smiled and walked on ahead.

That evening, they sat with their eyes closed, repeatedly stopping thoughts bothering them once they had appeared.

When they opened their eyes, Conor said. 'The stillness without thoughts is indescribable. I can't find words for it but it's the best I have ever felt, or experienced, the best sate of consciousness ever. I don't know what to say.'

'I don't know what to say either,' Lily said. It is not just inner peace, it is a sense of connectedness, of a oneness with everything.'

They had an early evening meal of vegetables and fruit from a nearby stall and slept soundly in their room.

◎

They woke an hour before dawn to walk in the cooler early morning air. Lily and Conor both immediately got on with their only task for the day. They were going up the hill to the cave to find out more.

On the way to the path up the mountain, they bought some more water and extra provisions. On the way back to the path, once again they noticed the same man walking in front of them. They did not want to disturb him again, so they walked slowly behind him at a distance until they came to the path up the mountain. He walked past the path but just before they turned up the mountain path, he stopped, turned around, looked at them with a serene smile and continued.

The way up the mountain felt a little easier than before and they realised they were getting used to the South Indian heat. As they slowly walked up between the rocks, they felt more relaxed about the man, the people in the cave and the mountain.

When they reached the opening of the cave, the two attendants came towards them from inside the cave. They moved apart from each other, standing either side to let them pass, bowing their heads in a respectful way. The man on the left recognised them and smiled, beckoned with his upturned hand for them to enter the cave.

The cave seemed to be waiting for them, welcoming them. There was something about feeling as if they had just got home from a long trip.

They walked into the cave, noticing more this time the light from the cave entrance being replaced by light from the simple oil lamps on top of rocks. They came to where the young man and woman who they had seen before had been and walked on.

As they continued walking into the cave, the light from the simple oil lamps on top of rocks seemed like guiding beacons. Eventually they came to the man who they had seen before and a little further they came to the woman they had also seen.

The attendant beckoned the Lily to sit in front of the woman who was sitting on the dusty floor of the cave. She was sitting against the wall of the cave in the position of someone meditating with her legs crossed.

◎

Lily accepted the invitation and sat several feet away with her back leaning against the opposite wall of the cave. She closed her eyes and sat with the woman.

The attendant then beckoned Conor to sit in front of the man who was sitting on the dusty floor of the cave. He was sitting against the wall of the cave in the position of someone meditating with his legs crossed.

Conor accepted the invitation and sat several feet away with his back leaning against the opposite wall of the cave. He closed his eyes and sat with the man.

After some time, the visitors opened their eyes when they heard the man and woman opposite them making sounds of movements.

The two visitors looked at the man and woman. It was as if there was an unspoken warmness of shared purpose between them.

Lily was the first to speak.

'Can you tell me more. I now see there is more to this. I want to know more about this. Can you show me?'

There was a long silence whilst words were found to express the answer. The man spoke slowly with long pauses between his words.

∞

'Most importantly, first you need to have simple mind control.'

∞

'You need to be able to keep thoughts away and to focus on one thing.'

∞

'This is mind control. It is effort.'

184

∞

'When you see how to control the mind, you begin to be more conscious of what you are.'

∞

'You see you are not your mind but something bigger.'

∞

'When you know how to control your mind with meditation, you begin to ask what you are.' Said the woman.

∞

'How do you find out?' Conor asked.

∞

'You see the Self inside yourself by yourself.'

∞

'Your nature is stillness.'

∞

'This state of consciousness is happiness.'

∞

'How do you see this?' Lily asked.

∞

'Our difficulty is seeing how simple it is.'

∞

'We are taught and conditioned by the world that we can be happy if we acquire all the things on offer, from material things to knowledge and power.'

∞

'Only when we see none of these make us happy, but lead to suffering, we start to unveil our inner self, and our ignorance of our true inner self is removed.'

∞

'How do you know this?' Conor asked the man.

∞

'You have to ask what you are, your whole life. That question must be at the forefront of your consciousness so that your happiness is your main priority.'

∞

'It is not that you have to keep on asking yourself the same question all the time, What am I? Who am I? But that you constantly try and be what you are and avoid what you are not.'

186

∞

'Making the effort to do this as often as you can, you see what you are.'

∞

'How do you know this?' Lily asked the woman.

∞

'We are only novices and have learnt from others.'

∞

After she said this, she turned away from the visitors and she beckoned the man to follower her back into the cave. They turned around to smile at the visitors and a few moments later were gone, back into the cave.

◎

After some time, they got up to return to the outside. Again, the way back to the entrance of the cave seemed much shorter than the way into the cave.

Once outside the cave, Lily and Conor opened their eyes fully and squinted at the bright daylight.

They sat down in the clearing outside the entrance to the cave to quench their thirst, shared one bottle of water and gave the other one to one of the attendants.

After opening their food supply for the day, they only ate a little before deciding to climb down the hill.

Wondering if the attendants would like the

remaining food, they offered it to the attendants who accepted it with a nod of gratitude.

Visiting the cave had taken most of the day but they were still surprised to see that the sun was now on the other side of the hill and was going to start to set on the horizon soon. They began their walk back down the hill. This seemed to take a much shorter time than before.

When they were back down on the road, they noticed the man who had given them directions up the hill and the room. He was walking in front of them. He turned to look at them, smiled and walked on ahead.

That evening, they sat with their eyes closed, repeatedly stopping thoughts bothering them once they had appeared.

Whilst they had their eyes shut Conor said, 'Let's focus on asking who we are as they suggested earlier.'

When they opened their eyes, neither could speak for a while. Lily spoke first. 'The consciousness of what I am, is seeing what I am not. I get what he said.'

'So, do I now,' Conor agreed. Thought is our big illusion.'

They had an early evening meal of vegetables and fruit from a nearby stall and slept soundly in their room.

◎

Lily and Conor felt excited about going to the cave and so they both immediately got on with their only task for the day. They were going up the hill to the cave find out more.

On the way to the path up the mountain, they bought some more water and extra provisions. On the way, once again they noticed the same man walking in front of them. They did not want to disturb him again, so they walked slowly behind him at a distance until they came to the path up the mountain. He walked past the path but just before they turned up the mountain path, he stopped, turned around, looked at them with a serene smile and continued.

The way up the mountain felt a little easier than before. As they slowly walked up between the rocks, they felt more relaxed about the man and the people in the cave.

When they reached the opening of the cave, the two attendants came towards them from inside the cave. They moved apart from each other, standing either side to let them pass, bowing their heads in a respectful way. The man on the left recognised them and smiled, then beckoned with his upturned hand for them to enter the cave.

It felt as if they were on the right path and achieving their goal because everything felt right about going into the cave.

They walked into the cave, noticing more this time the light from the cave entrance being replaced by light from the simple oil lamps on top of rocks. They came to where the young man and woman who they had seen before had been and walked on.

As they continued walking into the cave, the light from the simple oil lamps on top of rocks seemed like guiding beacons. Eventually they came to the man who they had seen before and a little further they came to the woman they had also seen.

The attendant beckoned Lily to sit in front of the woman who was sitting on the dusty floor of the cave. She was sitting against the wall of the cave in the position of someone meditating with her legs crossed.

◎

Lily accepted the invitation and sat several feet away with

her back leaning against the opposite wall of the cave. She closed her eyes and sat with the woman.

The attendant then beckoned Conor to sit in front of the man who was sitting on the dusty floor of the cave. He was sitting against the wall of the cave in the position of someone meditating with his legs crossed.

Conor accepted the invitation and sat several feet away with his back leaning against the opposite wall of the cave. He closed his eyes and sat with the man.

After some time, the visitors opened their eyes when they heard the man and woman opposite them
making sounds of movements.

The two visitors looked at the man and woman. It was as if there was an unspoken warmness of shared purpose between them.

Lily was the first to speak.

'Can you tell me more about how you can sit and be happy?'

There was a long silence whilst words were found to express the answer. The man spoke slowly with long pauses between his words.

∞

'Most importantly, you need to have simple mind control.' Said the man.

∞

'You need to be able to keep thoughts away and to focus on one thing.'

∞

'This is mind control. It is effort.'

∞

'When you see how to control the mind, you begin to be more conscious of what you are.'

∞

'You see you are not your mind but something bigger.'

∞

'When you know how to control your mind with meditation, you begin to ask what you are.'

∞

'How do you find out?' Conor asked the man.

∞

'You see the Self inside yourself by yourself.'

∞

'Your nature is stillness.'

∞

'This state of consciousness is happiness.'

∞

'How do you see this?' Lily asked the man.

∞

'Our difficulty is seeing how simple it is.'

∞

'We are taught and conditioned by the world that we can be happy if we acquire all the things on offer, from material things to knowledge and power.'

∞

'Only when we see none of these make us happy, but lead to suffering, we start to unveil our inner self, and our ignorance of our true inner self is removed.'

∞

'How do you know this?' Conor asked the man.

∞

'You have to ask what you are, your whole life. That question must be at the forefront of your consciousness so that your happiness is your main priority.'

∞

'It is not that you have to keep on asking yourself the same question all the time, What am I? Who am I? But that you constantly try and be what you are and avoid

192

what you are not.'

∞

'Making the effort to do this as often as you can, you see what you are.'

∞

'How do you know this?' Conor asked the man.

∞

'When you sit quietly with your eyes closed and you battle your thoughts so that they go, what is left is your consciousness without thoughts, the witness.'

∞

'When at other times you are active with your eyes open, do the same.'

∞

'You find out what you actually are by eliminating what you are not.'

∞

'Happiness is your only desire.'

∞

'To uncover this, you need to give up all else.'

∞

'You have learnt how to have much more control of your mind.'

∞

'When you have moments of stillness when there are no thoughts, ask what you are.'

∞

'You will see you are not your thoughts.'

∞

'You will see you are not a bundle of thoughts.'

∞

'You will see you are the witness of thoughts.'

∞

'Being conscious of being the witness is just being still.'

∞

'How do you know this?' Conor asked the woman.

∞

'We are only novices and have learnt from others.'

∞

When she said this, she beckoned the man to follower her back into the cave. They turned to smile at the visitors and a few moments later were gone, back into the cave.

Lily turned to see where the man and woman had gone then she turned to look back at Conor. She looked at him with a look he had never seen before. Lily looked radiant with a simple smile of knowing.

She turned once more and looked at the man and the woman who were walking further into the cave.

The man and woman stopped as if they sensed that Lily was looking at them. Then they turned to look at her.

Lily smiled with a serene look of happiness, then bent her head just slightly, as if to say, 'Thank you.'

◎

After some time, they got up to return to the outside. Again, the way back to the entrance of the cave seemed much shorter than the way into the cave.

Outside the cave, Conor and Lily opened their eyes fully and squinted at the bright daylight.

They sat down in the clearing outside the entrance to the cave to quench their thirst, shared one bottle of water and gave the other one to one of the attendants.

After opening their food supply for the day, they only ate a little before deciding to climb down the hill.

Wondering if the attendants would like the remaining food, they offered it to the attendants who accepted it with a nod of gratitude.

Visiting the cave had taken most of the day but they were surprised to see that the sun was now on the other side of the hill and was going to start to set on the horizon soon. They began the walk back down the hill. This seemed to take a much shorter time than before.

When they were back down on the road, they noticed the man who had given them directions up the hill and the room. He was walking in front of them. He turned to look at them, smiled and walked on ahead.

Back in their room Lily and Conor both felt something was happening to them in the cave. 'I won't be going up the Hill again.' Lily announced.

'I knew today you have everything it can give you.' Conor said smiling. 'I still have a way to go, so I must go back.

They sat for some time with their eyes closed, repeatedly stopping thoughts bothering them once they had appeared. They repeated what they had done before. They were focusing on asking what they were, who they were. They had already seen that they were not thoughts and were focusing on seeing their inner self as the witness.

They had an early evening meal of vegetables and fruit from a nearby stall and slept soundly in their room.

◎

Conor woke two hours before dawn. He was now going up the hill alone. He was going up the hill back to the cave to find out more.

Whilst Conor got ready, Lily sat in silence. She had no more questions. She sat with a serene look. She was still.

On the way to the path up the mountain, Conor bought some more water and extra provisions. On the way back to the path, once again he noticed the same man walking in front of him. He did not want to disturb him again, so he walked slowly behind him at a distance until he came to the path up the mountain. The man walked past the path but just before he turned up the mountain path, he stopped, turned around, looked at Conor with a serene smile and continued.

The way up the mountain felt a little easier than before. As he slowly walked up between the rocks, he felt more relaxed about the man and the people in the cave.

When Conor reached the opening of the cave, the attendant who came out to see him was an older man. He looked at the older man, then bowed his head in a respectful way. The older man recognised Conor, smiled and beckoned him in to follow.

He walked along the cave for some time, again noticing the light from the cave entrance being replaced by light from the simple oil lamps on top of rocks.

Conor felt he was on the right path and achieving his goal because everything felt right about going into the cave.

Conor walked into the cave, noticing this time the light from the cave entrance being replaced by light from the simple oil lamps on top of rocks seemed brighter. He came to where the young man and woman who they had seen before had been and walked on.

As he continued walking into the cave, the light from the simple oil lamps on top of rocks seemed like guiding beacons. Eventually he came to the man whom they had seen before.

The attendant then beckoned Conor to sit in front of the man who was sitting on the dusty floor of the cave. He was sitting against the wall of the cave in the position of someone meditating with his legs crossed.

Conor accepted the invitation and sat several feet

away with his back leaning against the opposite wall of the cave. He closed his eyes and sat with the man.

◎

After some time, when he heard the man opposite him making sounds of movements, Conor opened his eyes.

Conor looked at the man and it was as if there was an unspoken warmness of shared purpose between them.

Conor was the first to speak.

'I am still getting thoughts which stop me having peace.'

There was a long silence whilst words were found to express the answer. The man spoke slowly with long pauses between his words.

∞

'You might see you as being your memories. You might see you being your future dreams.'

∞

'These are just thoughts and not you.'

∞

'The past and future are not you.'

∞

'The past and future do not exist.'

∞

198

'Only your consciousness exists.'

∞

'Your consciousness can only exist in the present.'

∞

'Staying in the present shows thoughts of the past and future to be only thoughts.'

∞

'Keep on with this until you eliminate everything that you are not. Including your thoughts.'

∞

After some time, Conor got up to return to the outside. Again, the way back to the entrance of the cave seemed much shorter than the way into the cave.

◎

Once outside the cave, Conor opened his eyes fully and squinted at the bright daylight.

He sat down outside the entrance to the cave to quench his thirst. He had some of the water and gave the rest to one of the attendants. He got out the food supply for the day but didn't feel like eating before the climb down the hill. He wondered if the attendant would like the remaining food, so he offered it to the attendant who accepted it with a nod of gratitude.

Visiting the cave had taken most of the day but he was still surprised to see that the sun was now on the other side of the hill and was going to start to set on the horizon soon. He began the walk back down the hill. This seemed to take a much shorter time than before.

When he was back down on the road, Conor noticed the man who had given him directions up the hill and the room. He was walking in front of him. He turned to look at him, smiled and walked on ahead.

Back in their room, he told Lily his experience of being in the cave and what the man had said. After this, they sat with their eyes closed, repeatedly stopping thoughts bothering them once they had appeared. Afterwards, they sat in silence for some time enjoying the happiness they now had.

Then they had an early evening meal of vegetables and fruit from a nearby stall and slept soundly in their room.

◎

It was two hours before dawn when Conor woke but he got straight on with his only task of the day. He was going up the hill to the cave to find out more.

On the way to the path up the mountain, he bought some more water and extra provisions. On the way back to the path, once again he noticed the same man walking in front of him. He did not want to disturb him again, so he walked slowly behind him at a distance until he came to the path up the mountain. The man walked past the path but just before he turned up the mountain path, he stopped, turned around, looked at him with a serene smile and continued.

The way up the mountain felt a little easier than

before. As he slowly walked up between the rocks, he felt more relaxed about the man and the people in the cave.

When Conor reached the opening of the cave, the attendant who came out to see him was the older man. He looked at the older man, then bowed his head in a respectful way. The older man recognised Conor, smiled and beckoned him in to follow.

He walked along the cave for some time again noticing the light from the cave entrance being replaced by light from the simple oil lamps on top of rocks.

Conor knew he was on the right path and achieving his goal because everything felt right about going into the cave.

Conor walked into the cave, noticing this time the light from the cave entrance being replaced by light from the simple oil lamps on top of rocks seemed brighter. He came to where the young man and woman who they had seen before had been and walked on.

As he continued walking into the cave, the light from the simple oil lamps on top of rocks seemed like guiding beacons. Eventually he came to the man whom they had seen before.

The attendant then beckoned Conor to sit in front of the man who was sitting on the dusty floor of the cave. He was sitting against the wall of the cave in the position of someone meditating with his legs crossed.

Conor accepted the invitation and sat several feet away with his back leaning against the opposite wall of the cave. He closed his eyes and sat with the man.

◎

After some time, when he heard the man opposite him

making sounds of movements, Conor opened his eyes.

Conor looked at the man and it was as if there was an unspoken warmness of shared purpose between them.

Conor was the first to speak.

'I am still getting thoughts. But again, they are not really about anything. They disturb the calmness I have found.'

There was a long silence whilst words were found to express the answer. The man spoke slowly with long pauses between his words.

∞

'The calmness we find inside is stillness.'

∞

'It is our stillness. It is our very self.'

∞

'It is not possible to use words to describe it because everything about it is beyond words because it is our consciousness.'

∞

'When you look at a mountain, one of the most impressive things about it is not its size.'

∞

'The most impressive thing about a great mountain is not its height.'

202

∞

'What affects us the most is its stillness'.

∞

'Stillness is what the mountain shows us.'

∞

'It is stillness.'

∞

'When you look at the stars in the sky, you see it is us who are moving.'

∞

'They are still.'

∞

'Stillness is your nature too and that is what your happiness is.'

∞

After some time, Conor got up to return to the outside. Again, the way back to the entrance of the cave seemed much shorter than the way into the cave.

◎

Conor sat down outside the entrance to the cave to quench his thirst. He had some of the water and gave the rest to one of the attendants. He got out the food supply for the day but didn't feel like eating before the climb down the hill. He wondered if the attendants would like the remaining food, so he offered it to the attendants who accepted it with a nod of gratitude.

Visiting the cave had taken most of the day but he was still surprised to see that the sun was now on the other side of the hill and was going to start to set on the horizon soon. He began the walk back down the hill. This seemed to take a much shorter time than before.

Once outside the cave, Conor opened his eyes fully and squinted at the bright daylight.

When he was back down on the road, he noticed the man who had given them directions up the hill and the room. He was walking in front of him. He turned to look at him, smiled and walked on ahead.

Back in their room, Conor told Lily his experience of being in the cave and what the man had said. They sat with their eyes closed, repeatedly stopping thoughts bothering them once they had appeared.

When they opened their eyes, they sat in stillness, as they did with their eyes open.

Then they had an early evening meal of vegetables and fruit from a nearby stall and slept soundly in their room.

◎

The sun had not yet risen when Conor woke but he immediately got on with his only task for the day. He was excited about going up the hill and back into the cave to find out more.

On the way to the path up the mountain, he bought some more water and extra provisions.

On the way back to the path, once again he noticed the same man walking in front of him. He did not want to disturb him again, so he walked slowly behind him at a distance until he came to the path up the mountain.

The man walked past the path but just before he turned up the mountain path, he stopped, turned around, looked at him with a serene smile and continued. Conor felt there was something very special about this man but he could not find words for him.

The walk up the mountain felt a little easier than before. As he slowly walked up between the rocks, he felt more relaxed about the man and the people in the cave.

When Conor reached the opening of the cave, the attendant who came out to see him was the older man. He looked at the older man, then bowed his head in a respectful way. The older man recognised Conor, smiled and beckoned him in to follow.

He walked along the cave for some time again noticing the light from the cave entrance being replaced by light from the simple oil lamps on top of rocks.

Conor knew he was on the right path and achieving his goal because everything felt right about going into the cave.

Conor walked into the cave, noticing this time the light from the cave entrance being replaced by light from the simple oil lamps on top of rocks seemed brighter.

He came to where the young man and woman who they had seen before had been and walked on.

As he continued walking into the cave, the light from the simple oil lamps on top of rocks seemed like guiding beacons. Eventually he came to the man whom they had

205

seen before.

The attendant then beckoned Conor to sit in front of the man who was sitting on the dusty floor of the cave. He was sitting against the wall of the cave in the position of someone meditating with his legs crossed.

◎

Conor accepted the invitation and sat several feet away with his back leaning against the opposite wall of the cave. He closed his eyes and sat with the man.

After some time, when he heard the man opposite him making sounds of movements, Conor opened his eyes.

Conor looked at the man and it was as if there was an unspoken warmness of shared purpose between them.

Conor was the first to speak.

'I want to know more about consciousness.'

There was a long silence whilst words were found to express the answer. The man spoke slowly with long pauses between his words.

∞

'Our ancestors used to say different things about it such as, I am That, or That thou art or Be still and know that I am God.'

∞

'Essentially All is one, All is oneself and One is all.'

∞

'Unfortunately, the scriptures broadcast this out to

everyone in the hope that people would just believe it.'

∞

'Of course, it is possible to blindly believe, but blindly believing it is not knowing.'

∞

'Knowing can only be achieved by finding out for yourself, by yourself.'

∞

'All and self are no different. One is All.'

∞

After some time, he got up to return to the outside. Again, the way back to the entrance of the cave seemed much shorter than the way into the cave. Conor could not say why this was. He saw that although he seemed to notice time, it was not a thing that concerned him anymore.

◎

Once outside the cave, Conor opened his eyes fully and squinted at the bright daylight.

Conor sat down outside the entrance to the cave to quench his thirst. He had some of the water and gave the rest to one of the attendants. He got out the food supply for the day but didn't feel like eating before the climb down the hill. He wondered if the attendants would like the remaining food, so he offered it to the attendants who accepted it with a nod of gratitude.

He was surprised to see that the sun was now on the other side of the hill and was going to start to set on the horizon soon. He began the walk back down the hill. This seemed to take a much shorter time than before.

When he was back down on the road, he noticed the man who had given them directions up the hill and the room. He was walking in front of him. He stopped, turned to look at him, smiled and walked on ahead.

Back in their room, Conor told Lily his experience of being in the cave and what the man had said. Then they sat with their eyes closed, repeatedly stopping thoughts bothering them once they had appeared.

They now sat for longer with their eyes closed and also sat for some time with their eyes open. All the while staying in inner stillness.

For the second time, Conor noticed that it seemed an immeasurable amount of time had passed. He was not sure how long he had been sitting there with his eyes closed. He was not able to say if had been twenty minutes or an hour.

Again, he saw that although he seemed to notice time, it was not a thing that concerned him anymore.

When they opened their eyes, they had an early evening meal of vegetables and fruit from a nearby stall and slept soundly in their room.

◎

Conor was unsure if he was seeing everything. He felt as if he could see things clearer but felt stuck. An hour before dawn he got on with his only task for the day. He was going up the hill and back into the cave to find out more.

On the way to the path up the mountain, he bought

some more water and extra provisions. On the way back to the path, once again he noticed the same man walking in front of him. He did not want to disturb him again, so he walked slowly behind him at a distance until he came to the path up the mountain. The man walked past the path but just before he turned up the mountain path, stopped, turned around, looked at him with a serene smile and continued.

The walk up the mountain felt a little easier than before. As he slowly walked up between the rocks, he felt more relaxed about the man and the people in the cave.

Conor felt more positive about walking into the cave and as he walked further up the hill, he felt a happiness which was strange and familiar at the same time. It was something he knew.

When Conor reached the opening of the cave, the attendant who came out to see him was the older man. He looked at the older man, then bowed his head in a respectful way. The older man recognised Conor, smiled and beckoned him in to follow.

He walked along the cave for some time again noticing the light from the cave entrance being replaced by light from the simple oil lamps on top of rocks. Conor felt as if he were on the right path and achieving his goal because everything felt right about going into the cave.

He walked into the cave, noticing this time the light from the cave entrance being replaced by light from the simple oil lamps on top of rocks seemed brighter. He came to where the young man and woman who they had seen before had been and walked on.

As he continued walking into the cave, the light from the simple oil lamps on top of rocks seemed like guiding beacons. Eventually he came to the man whom they had seen before.

The attendant then beckoned Conor to sit in front of the man who was sitting on the dusty floor of the cave. He was sitting against the wall of the cave in the position of someone meditating with his legs crossed.

◎

Conor accepted the invitation and sat several feet away with his back leaning against the opposite wall of the cave. He closed his eyes and sat with the man.

After some time, when he heard the man opposite him making sounds of movements, Conor opened his eyes.

Conor looked at the man and it was as if there was an unspoken warmness of shared purpose between them.

Conor was the first to speak.

'I understand the words, "All is one." But I can't actually experience it.'

There was a long silence whilst words were found to express the answer. The man spoke slowly with long pauses between his words.

∞

'Giving up the world as you have seen it, giving up thoughts, giving up the body as you have seen it and giving up all scriptures lets you see and know, "All is your self," so you can just be it.'

∞

'But it is not giving up anything at all.'

∞

'Nothing is lost.

∞

'Nothing is gained either.'

∞

'It is simply uncovering what you had not seen about it.'

∞

'It is removing your ignorance about it.'

∞

'It is removing the darkness in you by lighting up what is there and seeing what you are.'

∞

'It is not adding something or removing something.'

∞

'It is simply seeing what is here.'

∞

After some time, Conor got up to return to the outside. This time the way back to the entrance of the cave seemed much longer than the way into the cave.

211

He stopped to try to work it out. He thought it might seem shorter when his mind was released from something and longer when he was thinking about something.

◎

Once outside the cave, Conor closed then opened his eyes, squinting at the bright daylight. It was too bright to see clearly.

Conor sat down outside the entrance to the cave to quench his thirst. He had some of the water and gave the rest to one of the attendants. He got out the food supply for the day but didn't feel like eating before the climb down the hill. He wondered if the attendants would like the remaining food, so he offered it to the attendants who accepted it with a nod of gratitude.

He was surprised to see that the sun was now on the other side of the hill and was going to start to set on the horizon soon. He began the walk back down the hill. This seemed to take a much shorter time than before.

When he was back down on the road, he noticed the man who had given them directions up the hill and the room. He was walking in front of him. He turned to look at him, smiled and walked on ahead.

Back in their room, Conor told Lily his experience of being in the cave and what the man had said. Then they sat with their eyes closed, repeatedly stopping thoughts bothering them once they had appeared.

Again, they sat in stillness, with their eyes closed and some of the time with their eyes open.

They had an early evening meal of vegetables and fruit from a nearby stall and slept soundly in their room.

◎

Conor woke in a determined mood and he was not sure why. Even though it was two hours before dawn, Conor immediately got on with his only task for the day. He was going back into the cave.

On the way to the path up the mountain, he bought some more water and extra provisions. On the way back to the path, once again he noticed the same man walking in front of him. He did not want to disturb him again, so he walked slowly behind him at a distance until he came to the path up the mountain. The man walked past the path but just before he turned up the mountain path, stopped, turned around, looked at him with a serene smile and continued.

The walk up the mountain felt a little easier than before. As he slowly walked up between the rocks, he felt more relaxed about the man and the people in the cave.

When Conor reached the opening of the cave, the attendant who came out to see him was the older man. He looked at the older man, then bowed his head in a respectful way. The older man recognised Conor, smiled and beckoned him in to follow.

He walked along the cave for some time again noticing the light from the cave entrance being replaced by light from the simple oil lamps on top of rocks.

Conor knew he was on the right path and achieving his goal because everything felt right about going into the cave.

He walked into the cave, noticing this time the light from the cave entrance being replaced by light from the simple oil lamps on top of rocks seemed brighter. He came to where the young man and woman who they had seen before had been and walked on.

As he continued walking into the cave, the light from

the simple oil lamps on top of rocks seemed like guiding beacons. Eventually he came to the man whom they had seen before.

The attendant then beckoned Conor to sit in front of the man who was sitting on the dusty floor of the cave. He was sitting against the wall of the cave in the position of someone meditating with his legs crossed.

Conor accepted the invitation and sat several feet away with his back leaning against the opposite wall of the cave. He closed his eyes and sat with the man.

◎

After some time, when he heard the man opposite him making sounds of movements, Conor opened his eyes.

Conor looked at the man and it was as if there was an unspoken warmness of shared purpose between them.

Conor was the first to speak.

'I feel and see myself as a separate person. I still seem distant from experiencing "Everything as one," I still see myself as separate.'

There was a long silence whilst words were found to express the answer. The man spoke slowly with long pauses between his words.

∞

'Meditation brings you to one pointedness of your consciousness.'

∞

'You see there is no division between consciousness in meditation and consciousness when your eyes are open.'

214

∞

'When you ask Who you are, you eventually see you are not thought.

∞

'When all else is removed you see your nature is consciousness of stillness.'

∞

'The world of separate individuals appears as a dream.'

∞

'You see all is one. You see there is no division.' 'You are only distracted by your thoughts.'

∞

'You see that you are the witness.'

∞

'This consciousness becomes the lens through which you see everything.'

∞

'Eventually consciousness of stillness becomes the state you return to when your thoughts stop and you disengage from thinking.'

∞

'It is your default state. It is your nature.'

∞

After some time, he got up to return to the outside. Again, the way back to the entrance of the cave seemed much shorter than the way into the cave.

Once outside the cave, Conor opened his eyes fully and squinted at the bright daylight.

Conor sat down outside the entrance to the cave to quench his thirst. He had some of the water and gave the rest to one of the attendants. He got out the food supply for the day but didn't feel like eating before the climb down the hill. He wondered if the attendants would like the remaining food, so he offered it to the attendants who accepted it with a nod of gratitude.

He was surprised to see that the sun was now on the other side of the hill and was going to start to set on the horizon soon. He began the walk back down the hill. This seemed to take a much shorter time than before.

When he was back down on the road, he noticed the man who had given them directions up the hill and the room. He was walking in front of him. He turned to look at him, smiled and walked on ahead.

Back in their room, Conor told Lily his experience of being in the cave and what the man had said. Then they sat with their eyes closed, repeatedly stopping thoughts bothering them once they had appeared.

They were spending more of every evening in stillness. They saw that what they had previously regarded as being difficult times with difficult thoughts, was slowly being consumed by their own stillness.

They had an early evening meal of vegetables and fruit from a nearby stall and slept soundly in their room.

◎

When Conor woke, he felt in a strange mood as if something was special about today. He sat for an hour before getting on with his only task for the day. He was going back to the cave to find out more.

On the way to the path up the mountain, he bought some more water and extra provisions. On the way back to the path, once again he noticed the same man walking in front of him. He did not want to disturb him again, so he walked slowly behind him at a distance until he came to the path up the mountain. The man walked past the path but just before he turned up the mountain path, he stopped, turned around, looked at him with a serene smile and continued.

The walk up the mountain felt a little easier than before. As he slowly walked up between the rocks, he felt more relaxed about the man and the people in the cave.

When Conor reached the opening of the cave, the attendant who came out to see him was the older man. He looked at the older man, then bowed his head in a respectful way. The older man recognised Conor, smiled and beckoned him in to follow.

He walked along the cave for some time again noticing the light from the cave entrance being replaced by light from the simple oil lamps on top of rocks.

Conor felt as if he were on the right path and achieving his goal because everything felt right about going into the cave.

217

Conor walked into the cave, noticing this time the light from the cave entrance being replaced by light from the simple oil lamps on top of rocks seemed brighter. He came to where the young man and woman who they had seen before had been and walked on.

As he continued walking into the cave, the light from the simple oil lamps on top of rocks seemed like guiding beacons. Eventually he came to the man whom they had seen before.

The attendant then beckoned Conor to sit in front of the man who was sitting on the dusty floor of the cave. He was sitting against the wall of the cave in the position of someone meditating with his legs crossed.

Conor accepted the invitation and sat several feet away with his back leaning against the opposite wall of the cave. He closed his eyes and sat with the man.

After some time, when he heard the man opposite him making sounds of movements, Conor opened his eyes.

Conor looked at the man and it was as if there was an unspoken warmness of shared purpose between them.

For the first time, Conor doubted if he should ask the question on his mind.

He had a sense that the answer to what he wanted to ask would be so simple that he might even feel foolish for asking the question. However, Conor felt he had to ask the question.

◎

Conor was the first to speak.

'I want to know more.'

There was a long silence whilst words were found to express the answer. The man spoke slowly with long pauses between his words.

218

∞

'You now have to let go of wanting to know.'

∞

'When you see there is nothing more to know, you can just be still.'

∞

'You have to let go of everything and just be still.'

∞

'Then when you ask Who you are, you can see what you are, that you are only consciousness.'

∞

'You see your consciousness is one and the same as the consciousness which the universe has.'

∞

'You are the consciousness of the universe.'

∞

'Your consciousness which is 'I am' is simply what everything else has too.'

∞

'You are the same as everything everywhere.'

∞

'By having no thoughts, by being still, you see that stillness is your nature.'

∞

'Stillness is being fully empty of thoughts.'

∞

'Happiness is the stillness of no thoughts.'

∞

'Consciousness is the happiness of stillness.'

∞

Conor had a smile of happiness and after some time, he got up to return to the outside.

He looked at the man and gave him a wide smile of happiness, nodding his head as if to say, 'Thank you.'

Again, the way back to the entrance of the cave seemed much shorter than the way into the cave.

Once outside the cave, Conor opened his eyes fully and squinted at the bright daylight.

Conor sat down outside the entrance to the cave to quench his thirst. He had some of the water and gave the rest to one of the attendants. He got out the food supply for the day but didn't feel like eating before the climb down the hill. He wondered if the attendants would like the remaining food, so he offered it to the attendants who accepted it with a nod of gratitude.

He was surprised to see that the sun was now on the other side of the hill and was going to start to set on the horizon soon. He began the walk back down the hill. This seemed to take a much shorter time than before.

When he was back down on the road, he walked towards the guest house to stay in for the night. After a short walk he noticed the man who had given them directions up the hill. He was walking in front of him. He turned to look at him, stopped, smiled with a serene look and walked on ahead.

Back in their room, Conor told Lily his experience of being in the cave and what the man had said. They sat at first with their eyes closed and then with them open. Then they had an early evening meal of vegetables and fruit from a nearby stall and slept soundly in their room.

◎

When he woke, again Conor thought there was something different about this day. Even though the sun had not yet risen, Conor immediately got on with his only task for the day. He was going to the cave.

The way up the mountain felt a little easier than before. He felt more relaxed about the man and the people in the cave.

He noticed that for the first time there was no attendant waiting for him at the entrance to the cave.

Again, there was a warm feeling as he walked into the cave. He was experiencing a coming together of something which seemed natural, but which he could find no words for. He didn't look for words for the feeling as he knew that words could not express what he was feeling. He recognised it was a oneness, a unity of something in himself which he had seen before.

He went along the cave for some time again noticing the light from the cave entrance being replaced by light from the simple oil lamps on top of rocks.

Conor knew for certain he was on the right path and he was achieving his goal because everything felt right about going into the cave.

He walked into the cave, noticing this time the light from the cave entrance being replaced by light from the simple oil lamps on top of rocks seemed brighter.

As he continued walking into the cave, the light from the simple oil lamps on top of rocks seemed like guiding beacons. Eventually he came to the man whom they had seen before.

Conor sat several feet away with his back leaning against the opposite wall of the cave. He closed his eyes and sat with the man.

After some time, when he heard the man opposite him making sounds of movements, Conor opened his eyes.

Conor looked at the man and it was as if there was an unspoken warmness of shared purpose between them. Neither spoke in words.

Conor sat with his eyes open and looked at the man. After some time, Conor closed his eyes again. He then saw that he was the same as this man. He could see no difference between them. He became conscious that this extended further, everywhere.

Conor opened his eyes when he heard the man making sounds of movements.

The man looked at Conor and there was an unspoken warmness of shared purpose between them. Conor had a smile of happiness and after some time, he got up to return to the outside. Again, the way back to the entrance of the cave seemed much shorter than the way into the cave.

Once outside the cave, the Conor opened his eyes fully and squinted at the bright daylight.

Back in their room, the Conor told the Lily his experience of being in the cave. Then they sat with their eyes closed, repeatedly stopping thoughts bothering them once they had appeared. Then they sat together with their eyes open, just being still.

Lily noticed the happiness which radiated from Conor's face.

They had an early evening meal of vegetables and fruit from a nearby stall and slept soundly in their room.

◎

When they woke, the sun had not yet risen but Conor got on with the only task for the day. He was going into the cave.

He remembered the man who he and the woman had noticed walking in front of them, and who they had followed slowly so as not to disturb him. He always turned around, stopping to look at them with a peaceful smile. He had shown them the way to the cave.

The journey to the cave felt easier and more natural than before. Conor felt more conscious of every step along the cave as he now knew the cave well. It had the unique feeling of home.

He went along the cave for some time, again noticing the light from the cave entrance being replaced by other light.

Further into the cave he came to where the young man and woman had sat and he went past this place and carried on.

Then he came to the place where he had sat with the man.

He settled sitting in the place where the man had sat and stayed sitting there.

After some time, Conor sat up to return to the outside. Again, he began making his way back to the entrance of the cave. The way out of the cave again seemed much shorter than the way into the cave.

Once outside the cave, the Conor opened his eyes fully and squinted at the light.

When he returned to the room, Conor and Lily sat in stillness. They could see the other was full of happiness.

They closed their eyes and sat in silence with their stillness. Then they sat with their eyes open in silence with their stillness.

They then had an early evening meal of vegetables and fruit from a nearby stall and slept soundly in their room.

◎

When they woke, the sun had not yet risen but Lily and Conor got on with their only task for the day. Both of them were going into the cave.

They remembered the man they had noticed walking in front of them, who they had followed slowly so as not to disturb him and who always turned around, stopping to look at them with a peaceful smile. He had shown them the way to the cave.

The journey to the cave felt easier and more natural than before. They felt more conscious of every step along the cave as they now knew the cave well. It had the unique feeling of home.

They went along the cave for some time, again noticing the light from the cave entrance being replaced by other light.

Soon they came to the place where Conor and Lily had seen the man and woman.

They settled down in that place. They sat with their eyes closed, repeatedly stopping thoughts bothering them once they had appeared. They sat in stillness, conscious of their happiness.

After some time, they sat up to return to the outside. Again, they began making their way back to the entrance of the cave. The way out of the cave again seemed much shorter than the way into the cave.

Once outside the cave, Lily and Conor opened their eyes fully and squinted at the light from their room.

◎

Later in the afternoon Lily and Conor decided to go back into the cave.

The journey to the cave felt easier and more natural than before. They felt especially conscious as they now knew the cave well. It was home.

They came to the place where they knew they were most their inner self and felt they never wanted to leave there.

They settled down and sat with their eyes closed, repeatedly stopping thoughts bothering them once they had appeared.

They sat in stillness, conscious of their happiness.

After some time, they decided to return to the outside. Opening their eyes, they squinted at the light from their room.

They had an early evening meal of vegetables and

fruit from a nearby stall and slept soundly in their room.

◎

In the morning they decided to go back into the cave.

The journey to the cave was simple and more natural than before. It was home. They closed their eyes.

They came to the place where they knew they were most their inner self.

They settled inside, in their happiness, sitting with their eyes closed, repeatedly stopping thoughts bothering them once they had appeared. They were still. They sat in stillness, conscious of their happiness.

After some time, Conor and Lily decided to return to the outside. They opened their eyes and squinted at the light from their room.

◎

That afternoon when they wanted to return to the cave, they closed their eyes and were there.

They settled inside, in their stillness, sitting with their eyes closed, repeatedly stopping thoughts bothering them once they had appeared.

They were still. But even though they were, they were acutely aware of everything going on around them.

They sat in stillness, conscious of their happiness and they were consumed by it.

After some time, Conor and Lily decided to return to the outside. They opened their eyes and squinted at the light from their room.

◎

That evening when they wanted to return to the cave, at first, they did not have to close their eyes. Then the cave needed more light, so they closed their eyes.

They settled inside, sitting with their eyes closed, repeatedly stopping thoughts bothering them once they had appeared. They were still. They sat in stillness, conscious of their happiness.

After some time, the middle-aged Conor and Lily decided to return to the outside. They opened their eyes and squinted at the light from their room.

They had an early evening meal of vegetables and fruit from a nearby stall then slept soundly in their room.

∞

∞

∞

∞

∞

∞

∞

∞

∞

∞